PUBLIC CRISIS AND LITERARY RESPONSE
THE ADJUSTMENT OF MODERN JEWISH LITERATURE

BOOKS BY LEON I. YUDKIN

Isaac Lamdan: A Study in Twentieth century Hebrew Poetry (1971)

Escape into Siege: A Survey of Israeli Literature Today (1974)

Jewish Writing and Identity in the Twentieth Century (1982)

1948 and After: Aspects of Israeli Fiction (1984)

On the Poetry of Uri Zvi Greenberg (in Hebrew, 1987)

Else Lasker Schüler: A Study in German Jewish Literature (1992)

Beyond Sequence: Current Israeli Fiction and its Context (1992)

A Home Within: Varieties of Jewish Expression in Modern Fiction (1996)

Edited

Modern Hebrew Literature in English Translation (1987)

Agnon: Texts and Contexts in English Translation (1988)

Hebrew Literature in the Wake of the Holocaust (1993)

Israeli Writers Consider the Outsider (1993)

Coedited (with Benjamin Tammuz)

Meetings with the Angel: Seven Stories from Israel (1973)

Leon I. Yudkin

PUBLIC CRISIS AND LITERARY RESPONSE
THE ADJUSTMENT OF MODERN JEWISH LITERATURE

SUGER PRESS
UNIVERISTÉ DE PARIS VIII

In association with
THE EUROPEAN JEWISH PUBLICATION SOCIETY
EJPS
LONDON

EJPS

The European Jewish Publications Society is a registered charity, which gives grants to assist in the publication and distribution of books relevant to Jewish literature, history, religion, philosophy, politics and culture.

LES ÉDITIONS SUGER/SUGER PRESS
UNIVERSITÉ DE PARIS VIII
15, RUE CATULIENNE
93200 SAINT-DENIS
FRANCE

To Mickey
For her continued encouragement and support

ACKNOWLEDGEMENTS

Parts of this book have appeared in somewhat different form in the following: *World Literature Today, Reeh, Encyclopaedia of the Novel, The Holocaust and the Text, Jewish Spirituality in Poland* and *Amel*. But, as is inevitable with such a complex subject, the material has been rethought and reshaped.

Many individuals and institutions have played a significant role in the creation and execution of the text, and I would particularly like to thank the staff of the Department of Hebrew and Jewish Studies at the Université de Paris VIII for their friendly cooperation and professionalism in the production. Although I have extensively drawn on many sources, any responsibility for errors or distortions are of course my own.

TABLE OF CONTENTS

PREFACE

Contact between the Jews and the world outside resulted, amongst other things, in the production of new types of literature, many of which relate to other media, such as pictorial Art, in order to reinforce representation and seek out further means of expression.

Here we seek to examine the etiology of recent and current phases of this process. Literature exists within an external framework, but it also stimulates its own line of development, through its own specifically literary expression. Thus, there emerges a literary history, side by side with other political and social histories.

The aim of this book is to explore the range of some of this literary expression in the 20th century. The writers who are discussed are either not well known (as in the case of those of the first wave of emigration to Palestine/Israel), are largely forgotten (as in the case of Edmond Fleg), or hardly known outside of Israel (as with Yoel Hoffmann). In other instances, new forms of expression are examined (as in the chapter on "Memorialisation"), or there is a reconsideration of accepted categories (see the chapter on Appelfeld). However, all the work is of major significance and huge merit and appeal.

The book constitutes a stage in my ongoing attempt at a reevaluation and reconsideration. It sets Hebrew literature in a broader context, beyond the confines of exclusively Hebrew writing, and its scope continues to plough the furrow of some of my earlier volumes, such as *Jewish Writing and Identity in the 20th Century* (1982) and *A Home Within* (1996). But it is also quite distinct from those two books. Here, I am making an attempt to present an account of current post-modern techniques of representation, and also see these writings, from various traditions and in various languages, in relation to each other.

The writings and their authors are not only set within a historical chronology, but also in relation to the contemporary scene. This is not in order to see how the literary work reflects history, but rather to examine the way in which literature recreates itself in order to be relevant to current understanding. We are always aware that works of literature have an absolute value, whatever the time or place of their origin. But we also bear an awareness of changing modes and a separate ongoing story, the story of literature. Why do certain modes come to the fore at certain times? Why does the writer implicitly express dissatisfaction with a particular manner of expression and elevate others, sometimes even inventing forms or transferring techniques initially belonging to another context? The implied argument here is that this is not only a response to history but can be an anticipation of a perception.

The Jews, although small in number as a totality, bear a very broad span of history. They have also been spread very broadly in geographical terms too. At no time has this been truer than in the twentieth century; the radical changes in demography bear strong witness to these shifts. The literature of the Jews, whether written in specifically "Jewish" languages such as Hebrew or Yiddish, or in other European languages, often expresses the generalised sensitivity of the age, heightened because of the peculiar acuity of the Jewish experience. This may express the typical or the avant-garde. It might even harbour a residual attachment to the past, and so to older forms. Any further generalisation would involve distortion. Jewish writing assumes the characteristics of the language group and national context from which it emerges, whilst still telling its own story. So each case has to be examined separately as well as contextually and consecutively.

That is what we are attempting here, in full awareness that this is only a very small part of a much larger and infinitely complex whole.

I

POLAND AS THE VENUE FOR THE CREATION
OF A YIDDISH MODERNISM

Intersection of History and Literature

No literary phenomenon better illustrates the mutual dependency of history and art than the new Yiddish poetry in Poland emerging from the conditions of the Great War. For the first time in history, a major armed conflict was conducted not just between specific antagonists or between professional armies, but over the entire globe, engulfing whole populations. This was not just a matter of conventional warfare for the rational purposes of political power or economic gain, but beyond that, within a range of subsidiary conflicts and enmities, an expression of total hostility. Public rules, to the extent that they had ever been observed, were changed. No-one within the existing alliances was free to select options or to be absolved from the fight.

And as for the Jewish populations, there existed another front. Divided as they were between nations and empires, and thus between the alliances, they also constituted an apparently discrete target for the hostile elements within both the major parties to the conflict. Anti-Semitism had evolved into waves of systematic pogroms in the last two decades of the nineteenth century, and these expanded further in the chaos of war, bresking the boundaries of limited conflict. Within what had been the Czarist Empire, new forces conducted civil campaigns against each other in the strife following the Bolshevik Revolution. Crushed between the Whites and the Reds,

15

the Jews faced destruction from both sides. And within the emergent nationalisms that succeeded empires, the Jews were found to belong to no single entity. A range of new groupings, associations and States expressed their new pride in their own identity, but the corollary was that the Jews were rejected, expelled and massacred, within all the territories of what had hitherto constituted the Pale of Settlement. Collective expressions of the results of all this were phenomena such as: on the one hand, emigration, the continuation of a huge movement that had begun with the first waves of pogroms in 1881. But then on the other hand, there were the Jewish forms of nationalism that both reacted against and were imitative of all the other nationalisms of Europe and beyond, as well as political realignments that sought to remedy the sick condition of mankind and effect reform.

So pervasive was the violence and the disorientation of the public mood that the artistic avant-garde sought to find an equivalent expression to the altered public consciousness in their own work. For one thing, it was felt by some that artists, including writers of course, could not leave their art on the fringes, as though it were an optional extra, unintegrated into the general feeling. Literature particularly, in its deployment of language, the medium of verbal and nuanced expression, should articulate what was truly urgent and deeply felt by the means of the most effective tools available. It could no longer afford the luxury of separate containment, finding fine form in traditional literary modes; it rather had to match the essence of the essentially human, in all its pain and ugliness.

So, as the Jews had not only borne the brunt of contemporary horror but a good bit extra too, the Jewish writer had a very specific obligation, in this understanding, to give voice to the specific condition of the Jew. And this had voice had to be couched in the appropriate terms, through the medium of the Jewish language. The spoken tongue that was common to the Jews of the ex Pale was Yiddish, that German derived argot, written in Hebrew characters, which had cultivated a personality and character of its own, becoming a separate and unique language, with its own modes and individual expression. Yiddish literature was the literature of the Pale and of the Jewish communities therein. It was marked out by its folk nature, its closeness to the language of speech, characterised by its self deprecating tone, its sense of being a minority at the mercy of the larger forces in operation. The classic writers, as well as the theorists, critics and historians of Yiddish, had crystallised standards of orthography and practice that had not been in force earlier in the sort of wayward anarchy that had been regarded as acceptable. Now, writers such as Mendele Moykher Sforim (1836-1917), Sholem Aleichem (1859-1916) and I.L. Peretz (1852-1915), had set standards of composition and form that established a literary base on which could be constructed an edifice of Yiddish literary development. Yiddish could henceforth be regarded as the legitimate language of a modern literature, taking its proper place on the world stage.

But by the time of the demise of these three classic founding fathers, all within the space of three years, and that within First World War, both world consciousness and literary consciousness had changed amongst the leading young practitioners. The new generation of writers had been born at the turn of the new century into a new world, and the literature that they sought to forge had to express this new world. From Wohlnia and Eastern Galicia, the poets, Melech Ravitch (1893-1976), Peretz Markish (1895-1952) and Uri Zvi Greenberg (1896-1983), met together in Warsaw in the early 1920s to form and consolidate a new tendency in Yiddish poetry. This was a conscious, even perhaps a self-conscious move, which both reflected the general movement of literary fashions throughout the world, and attempted to shape them for the specific needs, purposes and directions of the Jews.

Poland, and Warsaw in particular, of the first half of the decade, constituted a quintessential element in modern Jewish literature. It could only exist in that time and of that place. Poland was the primary centre of Jewish life, now of course rivalled by New York, but also, apparently preserving something of the traditional framework of community. Poland was a new Republic, and the Jews had a degree of cultural autonomy with Yiddish as its recognised language, spoken generally by the masses. Modernism had to succeed to the structures of tradition, which were falling, or had already collapsed. And yet, for reasons that are now clear, the phenomenon of this literary renaissance was also to be short lived. The towers of Yiddishism in Poland was to be toppled by the forces of economic crisis, hostile nationalisms and virulent anti-Semitism. This was to produce emigration, collapse and demise, in the shape both of a search for alternative structures of Jewish life and culture and the toppling of the old.

The Gang

Ravitch himself gives the primary account of the foundation of "The Gang" (*Khaliastre*) in his three volume autobiography, of which the second volume recounts the Warsaw years.[1] It is Ravitch who stresses the peculiar significance of Warsaw as a centre.[2] For him, Warsaw had been the city of Peretz, founding father and guiding light and inspiration of Yiddishism. It is Warsaw that has drawn him from Vienna, where he had been livng. Although Vienna was even more of a metropolis in general terms than Warsaw, it was Warsaw that he saw as the capital of the Jewish people in its actuality, and the repository of its cultural future. It is a fact too that the three modernist poets, Ravitch, Markish and Greenberg, were drawn there, all from elsewhere. They were to depart too for other, hopefully more welcoming venues, in accordance with their various and eventually disparate ideologies, Markish to the Soviet Union, where he was to be murdered in the Stalinist purges, Ravitch to Melbourne, and then on to Montreal, in search of a cosmopololitan Jewish environment, and Greenberg to Palestine/Israel, in fulfillment of his Zionist vision. But that, as they say, is another and later story. In the early 1920s, Poland was seen as the prime site for Jewish literary expression, with Warsaw as its capital and hub. It combined the virtues of containing the past and developing possibilities for the future: 'Religious, Jewish Poland following the First World War remained what it had been, but international Jewish Poland was beginning to develop in a

---

1. Melech Ravitch, *Dos maaseh buch fun main lebn*. Verlag I.L. Peretz. Tel Aviv, 1975. Vol.2.
2. Ibid. p.10, where he stresses how the three "alephs" of the name Warsaw have entered his soul and become part of him.

fast tempo.'[3] This applied to such Yiddish cultural institutions as; theatre, art, literature and schools.

This was combined with a sense of the historical moment. In the late Spring of 1922 for example, Ravitch observed the Jewish world in a state of enormous flux and transformation. There was a succession of enormous waves of emigration to the USA (although that too was to be abruptly curtailed by legislation a couple of years later), there had just been riots and what he called "pogroms" in Palestine (in which, for example, the great Hebrew writer, Brenner, had been murdered), and there had been a great civil war in the Soviet Union, succeded by a dictatorship. Many of the major Yiddish writers had emigrated to the West. But although the Western democracies appeared to be so amenable, for the Yiddish writer there was no periphery in the form of a vibrant Yiddish speaking community, with a degree of communality and autonomy. Such a periphery existed solely in Poland, in the Baltic lands and in Romania. And this existed, more than anywhere else in Poland, which was growing like a swamp after the rain.[4] It was to this haven that such as Markish came in search of publishing possibilities and a readership. And this applied to the overall Jewish population too: 'The great Yiddish masses from hundreds of villages were coming in search of culture, an international culture expressed in the only language that they knew, in Yiddish.'[5] Warsaw also held special attractions for Yiddish writers, as it had been the scene of operations for I.L. Peretz, and thus the focus of Yiddishism, of which Peretz had been the recognised leader and spokesman.

It is true that there had been some violence in the region. But, as Ravitch sees it, for Markish, the Lemberg (Lvov) pogrom of 1918 three years earlier, was nothing compared to the bloodbaths of 1917, 1918 and 1919, in the Ukraine. Markish, the passionate, full-bloodied poet, was exploding with colours: '[y]ellow, green, blue, red, mainly red. Sometimes it was the red of an overdone, idealised Bolshevism, and sometimes it was red with the blood of pogroms...'[6] The author

---

3. Ibid. p.68.
4. Ibid. p.88.
5. bid. p.88.
6. Ibid. pp.88, 89.

goes on to say that Markish had been seen by the critic, Zalman Reyzen, as a prophet, so Markish left Vilna, where he had been, and then found his way to Warsaw.[7] It was in Warsaw too that Markish published the collection of poems for which he had beome so famous, *Di kupe* (The Heap, 1921). Ravitch seems to adopt this characterisation of Markish as a prophet. It was the word of the prophet that the masses were awaiting: '[a]nd they were waiting for the New, the redemptive word. That was the redemptive word, the word of a prophet, the young prophet. Intelligent Jewish masses - were waiting for the prophet.'[8]

Ravitch sees the situation in Warsaw of the early 20s as a conjunction of two factors coming together, the feeders and the fed. The feeders, i.e. in this context, the writers, were looking for the instruments of their trade, the publishers, the journals, the prominence of the language, other writers, and above all, the readership. The fed, or those who were about to be fed, were hungering for the writes, for just that "redemptive word", the prophetic oracle, which function the youthful, expressive Markish could fulfil. But Markish was not the only such "prophet"; there was also Greenberg, who came in from Lemberg. Lemberg had been a province of Vienna, when Galicia, and it was now a province vis-à-vis Warsaw in the new Polish republic. Greenberg had been much affected by the war to which he had been conscripted as an Austrian, and by the dreadful pogroms which he had witnessed. His poetry, which he wrote both in Hebrew and in Yiddish, was also ripe for the new fashions, and Warsaw could be a more hospitable host for this sort of work than other parts of what had been the Austrian and Russian empires. In addition to its other virtues, Poland was noted for the preponderance of Jewish writers in the national language too.[9] It was in this atmosphere that these young lions of like mind congregated, and formed a group, known initially as "yung yiddish",[10] the group of young Yiddish writers. Moyshe Broderzon (1890-1956) described the group, himself included, as a

---

7. Ibid. p.89.
8. ibid. p.90.
9. Ibid. p.91.
10. There was a short-lived journal of that name that appeared in Lodz, 1919.

"freylekhe...*khaliastre*", i.e. a merry gang. The apparent derogation was thus gladly accepted as an accurate and positive appellation, particularly by Markish, who was so influential. But, and such is the nature of things, this clique was inevitably to confront hostility amongst others, and it was thus that it was regarded by them as a derogatory soubriquet "*Khaliastre*" was adopted to describe them. The term had long existed, but it now was applied to this group, who were categorised, in the journal, *Moment*, as a "gang (*Khaliastre*) of poets", originally coined by the well known poet Hillel Zeitlin, who was the journal's editor.[11]

The New Poetry

What distinguished these ideologically driven new authors was a sense of the new conditions faced by the writer in general, by the Yiddish writer specifically, and more than in any other form, in poetry particularly. But it was also marked out by the sense that new conditions should now be matched by new techniques, specifically new verse techniques in Yiddish guise. Ravitch, Markish and Greenberg composed both verse and programmatic prose, setting out their intentions. All three poets had literary organs to carry this material, and to offer the reader the message of the new.

This Yiddish poetry faithfully mirrors the Expressionist poetry of the period, both in theme and in technique. There is an emphasis on the subjective "I" of the poem, who pervades the described material, and whose being fills the text. This ego suffers, and expresses his suffering. The external world becomes incorporated into the being of the expressive artist, who exploits all means at his disposal to convey the heavily charged emotion to the reader. Thus too there is a stress on physicality. In contrast to Impressionism, which seeks to capture the fleeting vision, the transient impression of the outside world, whether of people, landscapes or events, Expressionism focuses on the inner space of the single narrative voice, the speaker who is also the one who feels. He emotes, and the

---

11. Ibid. p.92.

poetry is the expression of the emotion. This poetry can and often is supported by the total concomitant apparatus, the typographical elements, the art work in illustration, the concrete, physical appearance and feel of the text as it appears in the volume. Ravitch wrote a long poem, "gezang tsum mentshlekhn guf" (Song to the Human Body),[12] which later appeared in the poet's Expressionist collection, *Di fir zayten fun mayn velt* (The Four Sides of my World).[13] Technical "innovations" include such features as surrender of rhyme and regular metre. The poem, in its pursuit of emotional authenticity, attempts to shake off aesthetic artifice, and sees itself as imitating natural speech in its most extreme form. The moment of this surrender, (in Ravitch's case, 1921), is the moment of contact with universal violence, destruction and chaos. Eternal night is all around, but a window can still be opened out towards day: 'A day is just a strip of light in eternal night,/ And man is a worm in eternal night,/ And is eternally crawling looking for God.' The poem does not hesitate to invoke religious images, and even to speak of God quite intimately. And he then dares to place God on an equal footing with man: 'Their name is man,/[14] For the second and last time!/ The world is a two-God-world:/ Man and Jehova-/ Person – God.'[15] Man here is both the generality of mankind, but he becomes perceptible through the poet's own heightened emotional antennae. He, like his Biblical ancestors, is intimate relationship with the divine; presumably, the covenant is still valid, although that validity ay be hard to discern. But, as one who is party to the covenant, he can still address the Divine Being as a virtual equal. All the limbs of man, traditionally numbered as 248, are now united in God's name, and known as "man". These separate limbs, now united, can recreate a person in equal partnership, and an equal partner can demand rights.

Ravitch, one year later, in 1923, celebrates his own attainment of strength at the age of 30, in "piyutim tsu der zun" (Poems to the

---

12. First published in *Khaliastre*.
13. The volume appeared as a collection in 1929, Vilner farlag.
14. The word used for 'man' is *odom* (Hebrew), meaning both 'man' in the sense of mankind, and the proper noun, 'Adam'.
15. From "Gezang tsu mentshikhn guf", first published in 1922.

Sun).[16] Again the poet seeks unity of mind and body when he pleads for the opening 'of a door in the midst of darker night.' It is the thirty year old man, in the full flush of his newly discovered powers, that has the power to open the door. But he is also a man who bears the mark of Cain on his forehead. It is his poetry that is requested to emerge from the darkness into the sun, and to raise the man's (i.e. his own) body and soul, which are now a single entity. This is a form of resurrection. So we note a further characteristic of this mode; the tendency towards abstraction and personification. Poetry takes on the nature of a character who can be addressed. Light and dark move from their signification as epithets to the assumption of concrete personality. And such is the confident assurance of the youthful poet that he feels that he is the possessor of the strength to shift one in favour of the other. The poem is the rhetoric of persuasion. The terms and images deployed are large. The narrator is shocked by his experience, but all the more desperate for transformation. Not only must the darkness give way to the penetration of light, but fear must be replaced by joy, cold by warmth. The sun can offer all of these qualities, and that is why it is such an all encompassing image, containing both light and heat. The poet as a young man is also representative of qualities beyond his own extent. Youth represents the beginning, the potential, and indicates points further.

There are two addressees in this long and definitive poem; the sun and poetry itself. The sun is the object of desire, and poetry is the means of reaching the target. The sun is described as '[t]he impoverished bread of a poor man', and the narrator becomes ecstatic in its recall and in its praise: 'That have I possessed in my very depths,/ And that has become my call,/ My praise, my song, to you,/ My God, my sun.' The religious has become the mystical and the numinous, as all is contained in the ancient potency of the sun.

---

16. It is interesting that U.Z. Greenberg, three years later, adopted a similar image when he attained the age of 30, in his Hebrew collection, *Hagavrut haolah. Sdan.* Tel Aviv, 1926.

The Most Extreme Expressionism

One of the leading voices of the Movement towards Yiddish modernism, a spokesman as well as prolific and innovative poet and prose writer, was Peretz Markish. Of Ukrainian background (born in Polona, Wohlynia), he grew up in a stetl before being moved successively to Berdichev, Odessa and Moldavia, away from his parents. He was mobilised in the Great War to the Czarist army, and started to experience and to witness the barbarity and violence of slaughter and pogrom in the Ukraine. He had begun to write poetry in Russian already in 1910, but switched to Yiddish at the time of the revolution He regarded himself as a "Soviet" writer virtually from his debut, and published in the Kiev magazine, *aygens* in 1920, and in *der komunist,* in Kharkov, in the same year. Although he left Russia at the end of 1921 for Poland, he remained in contact with Soviet groups, as he was to do in all his forays abroad. In 1922 and 1923, he visited Paris, London and Palestine, and it is notable, in view of his declared ideology, that he was much enthused by the experience of this last. He declared that '[t]wo great things had been created in the world: the Russian Revolution and the Jewish settlement in Eretz Yisrael.[17] But it was the former that was to fire him more acutely, and to which he was to devote his energies. The Soviet revolution seemed to him to hold universal significance, and to have application for all peoples and conditions. Wherever he was to operate, he would bring the message of the new doctrine as it was being carried out in the land of Revolution. Although he again returned to Poland, he finally again found himself, and this time permanently, in the USSR, at the end of 1926. And it was here that he was to meet up with a spate of attacks, typically and significantly, by the Soviet Yiddish, "proletarian" critic, Litvakov, who notably in 1929, charged Markish with narrow nationalism, saying that '[h]is (i.e. Markish's) heroes are almost throughout, Jewish.'[18] Markish himself regarded such a charge as patently absurd, attempting to defuse the charge by the logic of a reply to the effect that, since the material dealt with Jews,

---

17. See ed. C. Shmeruk, *A spigl af a shtayn*. Verlag I.L. Peretz. Tel Aviv, 1964, p.752.
18. Ibid. pp. 754 & c.

in the main, it was natural that the figures portrayed should be Jewish. The converse would certainly hold good, would it not, for narrative pertaining to Russians. No-one would find it surprising that stories set in Russia, and concerning Russians, deal primarily with Russians. But logic was hardly to the point here, as later events would bear out. He was also accused, paradoxically, of what became known as "cosmopolitanism", as he had continued to maintain contact with Yiddish journals abroad, publishing in the Warsaw *Literarish bleter*. It was conveniently considered a betrayal to publish outside the borders of the Soviet Union, i.e. beyond the reaches of Soviet control.

But that is a later story. The Markish of Yiddish Expressionism is the Markish who came to literary fulfilment, and who found his distinctive voice and poetic mode in Poland. This was with the *Khaliastre* group, whose leading spokesman he became, and for the first issue of which he wrote an introduction. The journal was founded in the wake of both the First World War and the Civil War. The young contributors then had supped full of horror, violence, and that peculiar sort of murderous venom directed specifically against the Jews. Markish, as we have now seen, had been particularly schooled in this experience, and was looking for appropriate tools of expression to match up to what had now become life. Otherwise, literature was in danger of becoming irrelevant, and poetry would be doomed to a merely decorative function. So, in the first issue of *Khaliastre,* a journal that was only to go through two issues,[19] Markish wrote the introduction that was to become the poetic manifesto of the group. He proclaimed: 'On the stone wall of eternity is stretched out the crushed and bloodied head, electric head of the twentieth century, consumed by fire... The lights are not intended for us... We, like barefoot gipsies, steal away with abducted children... The dead in our wrecked cities command us to sing their song, the song of rebellion...And so we sing, with our lamp not that of beauty, but of shocked horror...Because of the war and the revolution we have become tense and nervous.'[20] So we have the leitmotifs of the

---

19. Warsaw, 1922.
20. An approximate rendering taken from Leon Yudkin, *Al shirat atsag*. Rubin Mass. Jerusalem, 1987, p.6.

Expressionist programme; that literature should match up to reality, that it should find the appropriate images of that reality, with its characteristic violence and quintessential horror, and that the old imagery, once common to the aesthetic of poetry should be abandoned in favour of the tone more suitable to the twentieth century. He goes on to highlight the corollary to the first half of the equation, i.e. that the chief subject of poetry now is to be the suffering "I" of the poem, the pain of the one experiencing that pain, the subject rather than the object. The language is extreme because the feeling is extreme, and it is the function of literature, in this view, to provide an adequate mirror of the poet's feeling.

Markish had already attempted precisely this in his practice. In his famous poem, *Fi kupe,* (A Heap), he had written a sort of "kaddish" (memorial prayer for the dead) over the slaughtered Jewish masses of the Ukraine, in September, 1921. His poetic technique here included some rhyme schmes. But they are jagged and broken up. He does play with the conjunction of disparate images; he refers, for example, to the '[d]ay of blood and honey.' He writes: 'My head knows no rest, it finds no ark,/[21] My heart has no liquid for its parched mouth. And he concludes this section with the refrain of, 'And live in your blood'. This is an implicit reference to the Hebrew poet Bialik's use of this same image in his protest poem, "On the Slaughter", written in 1903 in reaction to the Kishinev pogrom. But it is also an echo of the Biblical reference, which is the original source for both poems, where it is said that God addresses his holy city of Jerusalem in disgust: 'And I passed over you and saw you wallowing in your blood, whereupon I said to you' "live in your blood, and I said to you, live in your blood.'[22] But in the Biblical source, this statement is followed by a message of comfort: 'Then I passed over you and saw you, that your time was now a time of love, and I spread my wing over you, and covered your nakedness, and took an oath in your regard, and entered a covenant with you, saith the Lord, and you became mine. Then I washed you in water, and cleared your blood from you and bathed you in oil.'[23] There is no such message of

---

21. A clear reference to Noah's place of refuge from the flood, in the Biblical story.
22. *Ezekiel* 16:6.
23. Ibid. 16:8.

comfort in the Markish poem, just as there is no divine voice to be heard. The poem of Markish is an expression of pain and rage. The only comfort that may be found comes from beyond the confines of the poetic expression, in an ideology of presumed repair that would be offered the alteration of political circumstance to be effected by world revolution. But this is to be a revolution of human beings, by human beings, and for human beings.

Options in Language and Space

The three leading spokesmen of the Yiddish Expressionist Movement offer a rather neat set of ideological options. Although they came together in Warsaw, although they were of similar age, writing Yiddish poetry in a secular vein. all looking for new forms of expression, and rejecting the classical modes, they came to differ ideologically. And in fact, they went their separate ways.

This personal separation also exemplifies the ideological divide and the span of choices available to the Jew of the twenties. Ravitch eventually opted for internationalism, seeing Jewish expression as unbounded by borders between countries and not confined to political doctrines. Markish saw the future as necessarily directed by Soviet Communism, the beacon of hope in a benighted world. And Greenberg selected the specific nationalist and Jewish solution now being played out in Jewish Palestine, confirmed by the international community in the form of the League of Nations, and to be implemented by the British Mandatory government in place there.

This option also carried with it a change of orientation. Not only was he to shift geographically, and to recommend that move to the Jews of the world, he also had to shift physically and ideologically. He was to emigrate to Palestine, and to change his literary language permanently from Yiddish to Hebrew. He had been a bilingual poet from the outset, taking his first youthful steps in both languages in 1912, almost simultaneously.[24] But the choice of language was not a

---

24 See ed. H. Hever, *Uri Zvi Greenberg; taarukhah bimlot lo shmonim*. Hebrew University Library. Jerusalem, 1977, pp.8-9.

casual decision but based on ideological impulse, and the Zionist option was tied up with the adoption of Hebrew. Yiddish was the natural language of the people, but Hebrew was the language of the Jewish future.

But that choice still remained to be made. Greenberg had already become a widely published poet in both languages in all the best known journals before he moved to Warsaw from Lemberg (Lvov). Like Markish, he had also been conscripted, although in his case, it had been to the Austrian army. His experience was of the violence and cruelty associated with the dreadful war, and he personally had suffered with his family in the specific violence against the Jews. His earliest volumes of poetry had addressed itself to that subject, making the ideological point that it was the duty of the Yiddish writer not to ignore what was actually taking place.[25] The cruellest lesson he was to learn towards the end of the war with the redrawing of boundaries; Western Galicia was attached to Congress Poland, whereas Eastern Galicia became part of the Republic of the Ukraine. Poland bitterly opposed this arrangement, and although the Jews remained neutral, in Lvov, the Poles turned on them with fury. For Greenberg, this served as confirmation that there was no viable prospect for the Jewish communities in exile, and his very narrow escape became a symbol of Jewish fate, and served as a warning and pointer. Already in the immediate post-war years, the poet began to cultivate a new style and to dwell on the subjects emerging from that experience. As is the case with so much Expressionist writing, the writer sets the suffering subject and narrator at the heart of the poem. The art work becomes a kind of confession, in which the writer admits his impulsion towards revenge and violence.[26] He admits that he has been driven crazy, and in this crazed mood, he is tempted to seek out blind destruction, hitting out in all directions. The language of the poetry is here getting more extreme, the lines longer, and the imagery more abstract.

That is the beginning of this phase of his writing. Greenberg settles into his expressionist mode in the early 20s, when he seals his

---

25. Ibid. p.20.
26. See his early poems published in Hebrew, *Hatqufah* 10, 1921, pp. 439-453..

association with the other two members of the "gang". This also is marked by the publication of his third volume of Yiddish poetry, *Mefisto,*[27] a full-blooded Expressionist work. Here, he has abandoned rhyme and traditional metre. The eponymous central figure, Mephistopheles, represents all negativity. He is doubt writ large, gnawing away at authentic feeling: 'And Mephistopheles always comes out on top; doubting, constantly doubting.'[28] This devil does not believe in the authentic fascination of women, preferring isolation: 'With me, for example, Mephistopheles dug up the essence/ Of that female magic and all that love./ He called out to me in sacred, awe he uttered: nonsense!/ Turn over the most beautiful of cheeks, and you see live flesh./ Blue eyes? Heaven is bluer, deeper.'[29] The tempter here makes the point that what the individual can gain from his own unfettered experience is greater than what is imposed on him by a woman: 'The perfume of flowers is more intoxicating than love!/ And the Canticles poem is sweeter than Shulamit!/ Love,/ Women/ All is vanity.../ To be alone is the main thing!'[30] The devil is casting doubt on the quality of human life, and would replace it with the man made imitation and representation. Man suffers and winces, and Mephistopheles looks on sardonically, cynically beyond human suffering.

So Greenberg (Grinberg, as the transcription from the Yiddish has it) plunges himself into the thicket of human feeling, which is the object of his literary expression too. The function of modern writing is to capture the full extent of the suffering individual, in his contemporaneity, and in the peculiar Jewish situation which has highlighted the features of modern man, and concentrated them in the strange individual before us. It is the author who represents this general feeling, but it is the man himself who is held up to the reader for inspection. In his "Proclamation" to the periodical, *Albatross,* which he himself founded "for new poetry",[31] Greenberg raises the

---

27. Lemberg, 1921.
28. In U.Z. Greenberg, *Gezamelte verk.* Magnus Press, Hebrew University. Jerusalem, 1979. Vol.ll, p.325.
29. Ibid. p.324.
30. Ibid.
31. *Albatros,* Warsaw. September, 1922.

spectre of the '[l]one, homeless poets in the foreign lands amongst the various centres of extra-territorialist Jewry.' This is his subject, and that is himself. But, in addition, this has become the symbol of the new poetry. It is as though, not only has the world been transformed, but so too have the people in it, and so the spokesmen must be of this new kind, alienated, homeless and foreign. This is the Jew of the 1920s, and the relevant poet is the one who belongs to this category, and who articulates its sensitivities and needs in the most appropriate form. In this same "proclamation", he writes of a whole generation that is wounded. The image adopted by the poet to sum up this state, and to give the new journal its sign of recognition, is the albatross. That strange bird/animal can be an ill omen, as it was for Coleridge in "The Ancient Mariner", is the new poet. He is not only strange, but indeterminate too, half way between bird and animal, not entirely happy on land or in the air, sometimes hovering awkwardly above the seas. For Baudelaire, in the famous poem of that name, the poet is like an albatross in that it is "exiled". But its gigantic wings 'impede its movement' ('ses ailes de géant l'empêchent de marcher'). In this way the new poet does not really find himself at ease with the common run of humanity, and likewise, he moves, an ungainly creature between the species. Following the presentation of the situation, he comes to the conclusion: 'Therefore for what is cruel in the poem,/ Therefore for the chaotic in the picture,/ Therefore for the shout of the blood./ And for: the free expression of man, its nakedness overflowing with waves of blood.' We see all the traces of his poetic concern here, some of which remain his themes well beyond the Expressionist phase. We find the motifs of the isolation of the narrative voice, the "I" of the poem, the insistence on the supreme function of the poet, bordering on prophecy, and the frank portrayal of the suffering of this speaker, who is also a visionary.

Mefisto was hailed as the most authentic version of Jewish Expressionism hitherto, and in the second issue of *Albatros,* Greenberg broadened his canvass. Now he took up the subject of Jesus, for the poet an object of empathy in his national feeling and in his suffering. Jesus of Nazareth, for the poet, is the despised target of racial hatred, and, like the poet himself, he cries out in his moment of despair: "My God, my God, why have you abandoned me?" In another piece in the same issue of the journal, "Red Apples of the Trees of Sorrow" (royte epel fun vay-baymer), the poet presents a soldier during the Great War in the battle over Albania. There he happens upon a woman, and offers her his seed, suggesting that only this is the guarantee for the survival of a new generation, and that perhaps the figure of Jesus might emerge once more. This seemed to be too much for the Polish authorities, which banned the issue, as reported in moment,[32] because of the offence that this might cause Catholic believers. This also signalled the termination of Greenberg's Warsaw period, and hailed his renewed wanderings, this time to Berlin. It was here that he was to come into direct contact with some of the German voices in the Expressionist Movement. But Greenberg was not to stay there for long, as he was to fulfil his ambition of moving to the Land of Israel a year later. And, in any case, the Movement was in its final stages. The world atmosphere was changing, passing through post war enthusiasm and reconstruction to later economic crisis and eventual collapse, through to Fascism and Nazism. Greenberg was to convert, almost permanently, but certainly decisively, to becoming a Hebrew poet, and render a new spirit to the post-Bialik phase of Hebrew poetry.

The End of Yiddish Expressionism in Poland

It is not difficult to discern the causes of the end of such a Movement. The span was for one thing inherently limited, as the very modes of its articulation were bound to exhaust themselves. The high pitch, the abstraction, the extremism are all marked for a short although vigorous life. It is notable, obviously with the benefit of hindsight, that *Khaliastre* died more quickly than it was conceived and born. According to the most reliable observer, writing of course many years later, the group had never really solidified, going off in their separate directions: 'Just as it was born, so did the Group, known as *Khaliastre*, reach its demise. Thus it remained a significant episode in the history of recent Yiddish literature, but it was never

---

32. See *Moment*, 23 November, 1922.

31

really a solidified entity.'[33] In Ravitch's own words, it became a shadow without the substance behind it. But, apart from the fact that there was such a span of doctrines and purposes that could mitigate against longevity, there were other factors that were operative. One, as we have seen, is the nature of Expressionism itself, which, of its nature, must tend to burn itself out. Another factor stems from the personal biographies of those involved. Greenberg departed, first to Berlin, and then to the Land of Israel. Markish never really settled anywhere, until his beliefs drew him back to the USSR, where he remained and later perished in the 1952 Stalinist massacre of Jewish writers. And then the local situation deteriorated, and Ravitch was himself to leave for other climes not much later. The three poets of the group had much in common. They were of an age. They used the same language. They wanted to renew and refresh the literature in a secular context. They had all experienced the horrors of pogrom and war, and had each gone through military service. And they came together in Warsaw. But they were drawn in disparate directions by what they saw as the pull of the future, and this was eventually to split them asunder.

Although the three poets were united in their cooperation over *Khaliastre*, they each had their own particular journal in addition. The *Khaliastre* was specific to Markish, whose inspiration it was, who wrote the introduction, and who was responsible for much of the content. Greenberg then set up his *Albatros*, and Ravitch also founded a journal, *Di vog* (The Scale) in the same year. Whereas the first two were involved with passion, belief and ideology, Ravitch's paper declared itself open to all, and its function was '[t]o call to all Yiddish writers from the entire world to come to Warsaw, as it was the paradise for the Yiddish language and the great dawn of world Yiddish literature in miniature.'[34] But the overall picture that emerges is not of a solid and splendid renaissance of Yiddish literature in spite of the virtually simultaneous setting up of three literary Yiddish journals. *Khaliastre* saw only one issue before shifting to Paris, when just one further issue appeared. *Albatros* also only appeared once

33 Ravitch, *Der maaseh-buch...*, p.96.
34. Ibid. p.111.

before facing censorship, and even the all embracing *Di vog* appeared just three times.

What was common to all three poets? In Ravitch's view: 'What had been and what remained was a glowing love of Jewry, a fateful love of Jewry... It was this was love of the most exalted level that united the three.'[35] Ravitch notes this unity in the midst of the diversity of which he is fully aware. He says that of the three, Markish believed passionately in the Communist revolution, as a palliative for the unfortunate Jewish situation everywhere and as a world solution to social and economic injustice and inequality. Greenberg believed in the Zionist solution to the issue of Jewish ex-territorialism, and so left for Palestine, casting in his lot with the "yishuv", becoming their spokesman and prophet. Only Ravitch believed in the '[W]arsaw continuation', and he saw himself as the most conservative of the three.[36] But gradually the recognition that the Jewish world had virtually disappeared in the form that it had taken before the First World War, took hold. The *shteltlekh* had all but disppeared. In the words of the noted Polish language poet, Antony Slonimaski: 'No more, no more are there Jewish Shtetls in Poland.'[37] This line is also the title given to the biography of another of the great authors of the period and a founding member of *Khaliastre*, the fiction writer I.J. Singer (1893-1944), who entitled his memoir, *Of a World that is no More.*[38] This work, written late, and published in the last year of the author's life, is by no means a sentimental recall of what had been, and its author does not long for the revival of what is now long departed. Singer was a rationalist, drawn to socially corrective solutions, whilst writing with great psychological insight. But he does apparently feel the need to set up this literary memorial of a world that predated the First World War. But the memoir comes to an end at the time of his early childhood. Unlike Ravitch, Greenberg and Markish, he did not come to Poland

---

35. Ibid. p.417.
36. Ibid. p.418.
37. Ibid. p.117. This was originally written in Polish.
38. I.J. Singer, *Fun a velt vos is nishto mer.* Originally published under the title, *Emese pasirungen* (True Events), *Forverts*, April 15 - October 7, 1944. Translated as: *Of a World that is No More.* The Vanguard Press. New York, 1970.

from the outside. He was born and bred in Poland, born in Bilgoray, and reared in a Warsaw province. He lived in Poland until 1918, when he moved first to Kiev, and then in 1920 to Moscow, which had been taken over by the Bolsheviks. But in 1921, he returned to Warsaw, where he remained until 1933, when he departed for the USA as a renowned Yiddish writer. But, by then, the Yiddish world that had been, was no more, although it might have taken a while to appreciate its terminal demise. Again, in hindsight, perhaps the frenetic activity of 1922 is akin to the frenzied twitching of the chicken's carcass following its slaughter.

The phase of Yiddish Expressionism is brief but important. It is also unique in the annals of Yiddish literature. It remains the powerful and fruitful reaction to the circumstances of destruction and attempted rebirth. Even the variety of response within the limited span is testament to vitality. The great poetry and the vigorous prose in Yiddish found itself eventually without a hinterland and without sources of support in a readership that was either disappearing or assimilating into the new national cultures of the States emerging or being consolidated in the world's post imperial phase. What was emerging was a monolingual, single nation, Poland, a Poland without the Shtetl, and eventually without Jews, then an English speaking American Jewry, and a new Hebrew speaking Israel. But the modernism of the Yiddish Poland of the 1920s is a remarkable phase which produced an exciting literature, whose like we have not since witnessed, and of which we find imitations and echoes in later work.

II

THE SCORCH OF THE ORIENT:
HEBREW IMMIGRANT WRITERS OF THE 1ST. ALIYAH
AND THEIR ENCOUNTER WITH THE LAND

The First Aliyah

Following the fateful year of 1881, when Czar Alexander II of Russia was assassinated at the beginning of March, a wave of pogroms[1] hit the Russian Empire, numerically the greatest centre of World Jewry at that time. Although there had been sporadic attacks and intermittent outbreaks of violence before, as well as extensive restrictive legislation binding the Jews to residence in certain areas only (the so-called Pale of Settlement),[2] there was now heralded a new type of terror, broad in extent, calculated, systematic, and more sinister than that which preceded it.

---

1. The pogroms following on the assassination of Czar Alexander II began in earnest in April, 1881. See Jonathan Frankel. *Prophecy and Politics: Socialism, Nationalism, and the Russian Jews, 1862-1917*. Cambridge University Press. Cambridge, 1981, p.49 & c. The author there writes: 'It has been estimated that by the end of the year, pogroms had taken place in over two hundred towns and villages.' The "pogroms" proper had been confined to Southern Russia, although there was also considerable destruction in the North West, in such centres as Vitebsk, Pinsk, Minsk etc.

2. There had been increasing governmental hostility to the Jews before the assassination of Alexander II, but this now reached an unprecedented climax, see Salo Baron. *The Russian Jew under Tsars and Soviets*. Macmillan, New York. 2nd. ed. 1976. (1st. ed. published, 1964), pp.26-42. These difficulties were compounded by the further restrictions embodied in the so-called "May Laws" introduced in May, 1882, reducing the extent of the Pale of Settlement, thus forcing inhabitants out.

As a consequence, the Jews, in their turn had to seek a more enduring solution to their plight. Broadly speaking, for all the variations within, this comprised either reforming or revolutionising the conditions of Russia itself, or, on the other hand, getting out, i.e. emigrating. The former option would necessarily, within the authoritarian framework prevailing, put them in the banned, oppositionist camp. So it was the latter option that was embraced by an unprecedentedly large number of Jews, creating an enormous demographic change in the pattern of World Jewry. This consisted of an overall shift Westward. And this was a process that was to go on for the next four decades or so, certainly up until 1924, when immigration to the USA, the principal attraction, was virtually cut off as a possible future home for the would be settlers. At the same time, partly in response to the crisis, and partly as a consequence of an internally shaped demand for authentic self-expression, new tendencies were defined to formulate an equivalent of the breakaway nationalist movements all over the great, yet crumbling Empires of Britain, Turkey, Austria and Russia. The *Hibat Zion* (Love of Zion) was one such expression, seeking a revival of the ancient Hebrew culture in modern dress, and a return to the ancient Homeland of Israel, which was at that stage a territory of the Ottoman Empire. Although, in comparison with other emigrationist movements, this cultural, revivalist Movement was of modest proportions, later consequences were very significant. The Movement, despite all the drawbacks, disappointment, failures and disillusionments, was to lay the foundations for a new style Jewish settlement movement in Palestine that was to grow into a potential magnet for Hebrew self-expression, then later into a recognised Homeland (cf. the Balfour Declaration of 1917), and then into an independent Jewish State (the political entity of Israel, whose own declaration of independence was issued in May, 1948).

This emigration of Jews to Palestine became known popularly and in Zionist historiography as the first aliyah (lit. ascent), i.e. the first wave of Jewish emigration to Palestine in modern times, in the spirit of the new Jewish nationalism, proto-Zionist and Zionist. The dates suggested to cover this wave are 1882-1904,[3] from the time of the nationalist emigration in the wake of the assassination and the pogroms, up to the beginning of the second wave. In the course of this first wave, the yishuv[4] increased in numerical strength from 26,000 to 55,000 individuals.[5] Since the Land was so impoverished, disease ridden and generally inhospitable, those who selected this path were, on the whole, also those who were personally deprived, generally lacking in means, and from an unskilled and unmonied proletariat. The ideological thrust was in the direction of nation building, and, in recognition of the primitive condition of the Land, tended towards agriculture and land development. This was not only in accordance with the needs of the new country, but also in conformity with the thrust of the old country. Ideologically, the reformists allied themselves theoretically with the peasantry, and sought to develop an equivalent in Palestine. Tolstoy and his acolytes had communicated their passionate, reformist zeal to a new generation who saw in the crumbling conditions of Empire also the decaying fragments of effete postures.

For these settlers, two elements stood out. One was the new Land, and the second was the development of the actual material ground, the earth itself, which meant agriculture. The combination of the two came to be summarised in the slogan, "yishuv eretz yisrael" (settlement of the Land of Israel). It was the Hebrew lexicographer, Hebrew vernacular initiator and journalist, Eliezer Ben-Yehuda (1858-1922)[6], who expressed this quite early in his passionate and succinct fashion: 'Settlement of the Land of Israel; only this can save the whole people.'[7] Writing in Hebrew, the newly developing argot,

---

3. This is defined in (ed.) Mordechai Eliav. *Sefer haaliyah harishonah* (The First Aliyah), 2 vols. Yad Izhak Ben-Zvi. Jerusalem, 1981. Vol. 1, p.ix.
4. "Yishuv" (lit. settlement) is the term used for the Jewish settlement overall in Palestine.
5. See (ed.) Eliav, ibid.
6. Born Eliezer Perelman in Lithuania, he moved to Paris in 1878 to study Medicine so as to equip himself with a profession on emigration to Palestine. He wrote a seminal essay, "sheelah nikhbadah" (A Weighty Question) in 1879, advocating revival of the vernacular Hebrew language as a necessary adjunct to Jewish national revival. He arrived in Palestine in 1881, and thus can be reckoned as one of the first participants in the first wave. He remained in

which became his single minded obsession, Ben-Yehuda voiced the sense of frustration with the crumbling ramparts of the existing Jewish culture in the diaspora, as well as the need for a reconstructed entity focused on the ancient but renewed homeland, built on a renewed economic basis, and to be expressed in its own ancient and renewed tongue. In the Palestine of that period, he recognised the difficulties, the frailties and failures in the Land, but nonetheless, saw no alternative possibility for national construction.

Thus when we speak of the first aliyah and the new settlement, we use these terms in contrast to the old settlement and in recognition of a new page to be turned in the book of Jewish history. Certainly, the participants themselves, and specifically their vocal representatives, could only accept their very real sacrifices and hardship in the consciousness of creating something new and permanent. Diaspora existence was perceived to be secondary, contingent and transitory, subject to the passing whims of the host society. A new Palestine could be, if sufficiently nurtured, an authentic, independent creation. The overall achievement of this wave may be essentially modest in overall numerical terms, but it set a trend that was to become a continuing process, despite the fallout and failure on the way.

Four bodies contributed to the seven individual settlements that were set up in the course of this period. One, which we have mentioned, was the "Hibat zion" (Love of Zion) Movement. The second reformist movement was "bilu"[8], advocating a national, socialist ideology, from the very early 80s of the century. The third element was the Rothschild settlements, supported by the banking family for charitable purposes and for the production of wine. And the fourth was the "old yishuv", that is, the pre-existing settlements of a strongly orthodox tendency, far removed from the infectious spirit of change being spread by this quasi nationalistic reformism.

Palestine basically until his death, apart from the duration of the war, when he he had to leave as a journalist because of the Ottoman censorship.

7. See *Havatzelet*, issue 42. Jerusalem, 6 September, 1879.

8. This is a Hebrew acronym for "bet yaaqov lekhu venelkhah" (house of Jacob, come let us go), a phrase which was adopted as the motto of the group, indicating its concern with emigration and return to the Land.

But we must be wary of seeing even this 22 year span as constituting a unitary character. During the late 80s, there was a period of retrenchment and fallout, when the Turkish rulers resisted the "intruders", and yet, despite this, in 1900, the ICA (Jewish Colonisation Association) was set up to assist and support further settlement ventures. By this later time of course, the World Zionist Organisation (WZO) had been conceived and created, and one of its main purposes was the promotion of agricultural settlement in the Land, and its preparation for future absorption of population.[9] This element was taken up and developed much further by the members of the second aliyah, in 1904 and beyond, when they founded 28 new agricultural settlements. Agriculture, and later, collectivist agriculture, was to become the fundamental ideological characteristic of Zionist settlement, supported politically by various Labour parties, which were to dominate Israeli politics until 1977. It was in that year that the right wing, *Likud* party, became the principal faction in the Israeli government.

Pioneering emigration to Palestine was by no means an easy option. Even for those who had been totally without means in the old countries, Palestine came to be seen as a remarkably tough alternative. The imperial government was basically hostile to and suspicious of the interlopers. The local inhabitants, the Arab population also regarded the immigrants as alien. The soil was not very fertile, and the climate extreme and unmanageable. Terrible disease was endemic in the region. Palestine was an economic backwater, and communication with Europe was poor. Altogether, the situation for new settlers was very unpromising, so that the stimulus required to make the effort to be integrated had to be correspondingly substantial. Either there had to be an extreme reaction to the hostility of the place of origin, or an extraordinarily positive impulse towards the ancestral territory. Preferably, both factors had to come into play, and these were augmented by some sort of financial and social assistance.

---

9. This became a basic plank of official Zionist policy despite Herzl's initial objection to piecemeal infiltration, and his own preference for political solutions in the direction of a "charter".

We can see a typical early reaction in the words of Zalman David Levontin (1856-1940), when he describes the founding of one of the early colonies, Rishon Lezion.[10] He bemoans both the physical and the spiritual load that he has to take on, and also laments the isolation in which he finds himself. We may speak now of this wave as a significant historical phenomenon, but the number involved were pitifully small: 'My brethren, where are they?' he asks, knowing that the answer, however unspecific , must be in the nature of; 'in any case, not here.' He continues rhetorically: 'Am I capable of bearing on one of my shoulders sheaves of wheat, and on the other the load of this people that is with me, together with its burden?' Most of these soi-disant farmers had no previous experience of agriculture, coming as they did, in the main, from the communities of the Russian Pale of Settlement and the small villages of Romania. On the whole, they had been petty traders and small shopkeepers, and a lot of their work disguised virtual unemployment. The impulse to engage in this new sort of enterprise on unknown soil was the negative need to be distanced from the ravages of the Pale, and the attraction, idealistic or religious, of the ancient source.

The Literature

Given the necessary difficulties of acclimatisation, the sheer problems of existence, on the one hand, and the meagreness of the population totals within this wave of immigration on the other, one might not have expected here a great volume of literary expression. Add to this the difficulties of printing, the undeveloped character of the publishing scene, and the relatively brief time span under discussion, one might have thought that literature could easily not feature at all on the cultural horizon. Also, there was a particular problem in regard to Hebrew. This language was hardly spoken, even in this new centre which was ideologically committed to the language revival. Hebrew had been used regularly as a vehicle only for certain types of literature, and hardly at all in everyday conversation. This

---

10. See *Sefer haaliyah harishonah*, vol.2, pp.33-4, "Yisud rishon letziyon".

made natural and normal expression in the language rather problematic and self-conscious. The language had to be recreated and reinvented, the stock of vocabulary enlarged, experiments made with calques from other languages, especially Yiddish. So that altogether, the line of literary expression was not altogether smooth.

Nevertheless, Hebrew did make the necessary effort to reform itself, perhaps not only in spite of the problems, but even because of them. Literature was an inherent component of the total, nationalist exercise. It is reckoned that 22 periodicals were created in this period.[11] In terms of volumes of Hebrew writing produced, there were about eight known writers, in the sense of *belles lettres.* The first volumes started to appear in the second decade of the wave, at around 1890. In trying to characterise the overall nature of this body of literature, we discern links with both earlier and contemporary Hebrew literature. But there were divergences as well. Clearly, this literature emerges, as do the writers themselves, from the background of the Hebrew Enlightenment, the *haskalah.* They sought to convey what had been garnered from European civilisation to the Jewish world, to bring the people up to date intellectually and socially, and generally to use literature as a didactic vehicle. The very instrument of communication itself became part of the message. Hebrew was not only the object of the exercise, but also the subject, and, in its rendition, the instrument of advancement, learning and culture. We can see this in the Palestinian literature too. There had also existed another more recent tendency, in the so-called "Love of Zion" literature, which expressed a sentimental yearning for return to the Land. But of course, this was expressed from afar, without knowledge of the specifics of local conditions. These two tendencies were taken over into the literature of the first aliyah. But this corpus must also be distinguished from its successor literature, that of the

---

11. See Yaffa Berlowitz, "Sifrut ivrit bitqufat haaliyah harishonah" (Hebrew Literature in the Period of the First Aliyah) in *Sefer haaliyah harishonah,* vol.1, pp.447-464. The author also deals with the issue of the specifically innovative tendency of this literature in its view of the "new Hebrew" as one who not only belongs to his people, but has also been reunited with the Land, (see her book, *Lehamtsiy erets lehamtsiy am; sifrut haaliyah harishonah.* Hakibbuts hameuhad. Tel Aviv, 1996, throughout. .

second aliyah. This latter was, surprisingly, already hard-bitten, realistic, and even bitter, perhaps in reaction to the naïve idealisation of the earlier tendency.

So the first aliyah literature carries forward the lessons of the Enlightenment, seeing itself as having a national, collective and proclamatory function. Its regard for the Hebrew language enshrines the ancient values embodied within the classical and holy tongue. It also seeks out collective solutions for the problems of the Jewish nation, which it sees as unitary. Clearly too, it not only continues the line of attachment to the ancient land, but it also embodies it by relocating within it. However, it necessarily diverges from it by the primary contact with the Land. This Land is no longer a distant and unattainable vision, but a present reality. But, on the other hand, the literature has not achieved the natural and direct contact that is more characteristic of what was to come later. The distinctive feature of this body of work is that it is both within the tradition of the Modern, attached to the return and propagating it, but also distanced from its natural features. This has been summed up as "naively romantic" rather than that of the later's "sober realistic".[12]

One of the writers who first published was Zeev (Wolf) Jawitz (1847-1924). He was one of the founder members of "Hibat Zion" in Poland, his country of origin, and when he arrived in Palestine in 1887, intent on pursuing his ideals, he wanted to engage in farming. He spent one year and a half in the colony, Yehud, and then went to Zikhron Yaakov, which was, as the name suggests, one of the Rothschild settlements. So his acquaintance with the Land was first hand, direct and unmediated. Yet his accounts of his experience, first published in 1891,[13] are far from being a naturalistic and factual account of the place, its conditions and its atmosphere, as seen through European eyes. Of Jerusalem he says on his arrival: 'Before your greatness I stand in awe. I am moved within...you are still grand, still exalted, but how dilapidated...Zion has become a desert, Jerusalem a wasteland, and my heart and my garments are in

---

12. Ibid.
13. "Lashut baaretz" in *Haaretz*, (a one off anthology, originally intended as a journal). Jerusalem, 1891. Later published in "Mimarot haaretz" in *Leqet ktavim*. Mosad harav kook. Jerusalem, 1943.

tatters.'[14] The author here builds his narrative around the seasons and festivals, and he does not forget to impart his lesson. The Jews should come here, because they will, as a result, become healthier and more upstanding: 'The young men of Israel will toughen their arms and serve as a model for their brethren, of whom it is said: who are these infirm? They are the sons of Israel that have gone in to exile, that since their exile from Jerusalem, they have not stood erect. For which reason, I always think that raising up our sons to being courageous of heart and strong of hand is the first condition for permanent and lasting settlement.'[15] So our author both recognises the difficulty of his task and the reality of the conditions, but he presents both with an admixture of didacticism and good counsel, within what looks like the Enlightenment frame, now linked to the doctrine of *aliyah*.

The Hebrew Press

Hebrew journalism is as old as Modern Hebrew Literature, and in fact it was one of the instruments of its formation. From the mid-eighteenth century onwards, the enlighteners tried to forge both a new Hebrew literature and a receptive readership. But the task was exceedingly difficult. There were very few Hebrew readers in the whole of Europe, East and West, and they had to be cultivated. The first efforts were therefore brief and abortive. But gradually, as the Enlightenment spread Eastward, where the communities were more substantial, the readership of this material grew, and the journals became more regular, from what had been sporadic journals, to monthlies, weeklies, and even dailies. From 1866, *Hamelitz* (The Interpreter) in St. Petersburg, the first Hebrew newspaper, began to appear daily. Its ambition was both to cover the whole Jewish world, and to reach all its potential readers. Within the same decade, in 1863, two Hebrew papers were established in Jerusalem, *Halevanon* (The Lebanon, 1863-1886) and *Havatzelet* (The Rose, 1863-1911).

---

14. Ibid.
15. Ibid. p. 46.

Both of these papers proclaimed it as their function to communicate what was going on in the Holy Land to its readers, hopefully a broad span of the international Jewish community.

It was with this band of publishing outlets that the Hebrew writers of the first wave of the new *yishuv* associated, and where they had to promulgate their material. But we can also see from all this that the mere fact of journal and newspaper publication was not in itself an innovation. Whatever specifically marked out the new settlement, it was not just the existence of secular publication in the Holy Land. And, as far as the Hebrew newspapers of Europe were concerned, the link with Palestine was obviously crucial. This wave of emigration was boosted by support from Russia and the West; that was where its ideological roots were embedded. But the papers, their contributors and their editors, had a complex set of loyalties and obligations. The editor of *Hamelitz*, Alexander Zederbaum (1816-1893), for example, had to receive a special permit to publish this paper, in 1860. He later founded and edited a Yiddish paper, *Qol mvaser* (Voice of the Announcer), which first ran from 1871-1873, and was later renewed in 1878. He also had produced a newspaper in Russian, which was transferred to other staff, and continued under the name of *Razsvet*.

It seemed to be that his primary attachment was to the Hebrew paper, which he not only edited, but for which he wrote numerous long articles under the pen name of Erez. He began to support the Zion movement very early, as a cultural Hebraist. But his local aspiration was to preserve reasonable conditions for the Jews in the diaspora. The assassination of Czar Alexander II was a terrible blow to the spokesmen of Jewry, not only in itself, but for the perceptible danger that was implicit in consequence. The first thing to be done was to declare great sorrow at the "horror" of the deed and loyalty to the government, and, thus, to the Czar's successor. The problem faced here was one already familiar, that of dual loyalty. But there is no contradiction in '...holding together different national feelings, the nation of origin and the nation of birthplace, where such joint sentiments we perceive amongst other nations too, as they may be held in various countries. Who then can cry out against the Jews, if, whilst fulfilling all their obligations to the land of their birth as loyal sons, they also evince sympathy towards the place of their original holy stock?'[16] The argument is drawn even further, with the implication that one loyalty actually strengthens the other. What made the argument so particularly pressing was the tide of unprecedented violence that was to be unleashed against Jewish communities on such a broad scale. This constituted a national crisis rather than a series of isolated incidents. On a more theoretical level, the Jews had to defend themselves against charges of cosmopolitanism, a multiple attachment leading to disloyalty to their country of origin and residence. So, an appeal went out to government for a policy of enlightenment and tolerance, whilst attacks were launched simultaneously against the Jewish underworld for bringing the community as a whole into disrepute.[17] The paper argued that Jews should have rights equal with everyone else, but that they should also share in the burden of obligations. Similarly, Jewish spokesmen were nervous about forced expulsion, whilst they also insisted on full and equal opportunities for voluntary emigration.

The pogroms continued for many months, wreaking havoc to the sense of confidence within the community. It is thus easy to see the reasons for the mass exodus of the Jewish population at this time. Historians have indicated that, in fact, this trend was initiated earlier, both in terms of increased governmental hostility towards the Jews and in terms of emigration patterns.[18] But the tendency was reinforced, and, in any case, what looked as though it could have been sporadic and incidental violence began to take on the appearance of systematic and sustained persecution. In response, what had been piecemeal and individual abandonment began to assume various systematic patterns of organisation. The existing Palestinian channels assisted those who took the plunge, and threw in their lot with the *yishuv*. But the difficulties remained, as noted in reports to the paper.[19] There was a serious lack of water, oppressive and unbearable heat, and bad roads. The colonies did not appear to offer profitable investment, certainly not in comparison with what

16. See *Hamelitz*, issue dated 14 April, 1881.
17. Ibid. See issue of 26 May, 1881.
18. See Baron op. cit. pp.26-42.
19. See the report by Dov Ber Steinhart in *Hamelitz*, 8 September, 1881.

might be obtained from the orchards. Others advised those already thinking of emigrating to hold out no prospect other than in the Holy Land, as to go to the USA, for example, was to invite religious and cultural assimilation.[20] The editorial sharply denies the implications of necessary assimilation, forced or voluntary, in the USA, arguing that new institutions and frameworks were being set up for the immigrants there.

What we have seen from the editorial representation of the central Hebrew newspaper indicates a policy of holding all the options open. Free choice should be offered universally to Jews, whether for staying in Russia or in choosing to emigrate. In the selection of a place of emigration, maximal facilities should be created and sustained as a support system for the preservation of the cultural heritage. Loyalty should be evinced towards the lands of residence, and, specifically, in support of policies of liberalism; the assassination of the previous Czar was to be labelled a disaster, both in itself and in its implications for the Jewish polity. But still, return to Zion was a truly honourable option, and expressed the hopes of a revived Hebraism in the only place where that was truly possible. This belief in the preservation of multiple options continued as long as the paper lasted (until 1903), until indeed the atmosphere changed, and the choices became more focused and preclusive.

Moshe Smilansky (1874-1953)

Smilansky was perhaps the most representative writer of this wave in a very literal sense. He genuinely attempted to represent the collective sentiment of the immigrants; why they immigrated, what their aspirations were, what their difficulties were, and how they did their best to come to terms with them. He was an active pioneer, an agriculturalist, who not only believed in the project of return to the land, but also acted on it in his own life, and he was also a writer, who faithfully recorded the struggle, personal and joint. Most of the information that we have about him comes from the six-volume

---

20. See piece by Yehiel Heller of Pinsk, in *Hamelitz*, 22 September, 1881.

fictionalised autobiography that he finally published late in life. This consists of a very thinly disguised account of himself, set in the Ukraine and in Palestine, following the fortunes of "Yehuda" (clearly the author himself), from birth and throughout his whole life, the far greater part of which was lived in the Land of Israel. He came to Palestine in 1890,[21] and published his first article in 1898, following which, he wrote regularly in the international and Palestinian Hebrew press.

Smilansky is so important for our theme here because, in all his work: fictionalised autobiography, stories and articles, he deals with the situation of the Jewish immigrant to Palestine at this very early stage. He charts the sensation of first and, naturally primary contact with the Land in all its manifestations. His Ukrainian background is intensely relevant. It was formative ideologically, educationally, historically, and it also served him in a practical sense. He drew from it his attachment to nature, to the countryside, (as he worked with his father on their farm). He derived the ideal of horsemanship too from his Ukrainian childhood, and it also served him in good stead in later life. In this, he was not quite typical of his Jewish cohorts, but he felt urged to be able at least to equal his non-Jewish contemporaries, all of whom could manage a horse.[22] He was typical of the new spirit of the age, educated in the "enlightened" manner, learning languages, and open to general European influences. Part of the "new" in this respect was the systematic learning of Hebrew from a proper teacher in the same respectable manner as he learned Russian, not just by rote, in the crabbed, traditional fashion. He was influenced too by the "Lovers of Zion", and, in particular, by the writers amongst them, such as Smolenskin and Lilienblum. More specifically, he was drawn to the accounts of first settlement in Palestine, '...about Rishon Lezion, about Gedera, and how their builders ascended their desolate hills at the first', when he heard such accounts from welcome emissaries. He began to ask the questions characteristic of the proto-Zionists and Zionists, such as why the Jews are not farmers in Russia, and why they do not defend themselves in the pogroms. Intellectu-

---

21. Kressel gives his Hebrew date of aliyah as Cheshvan, 5651, which year is the equivalent of 1890-1, see G.Kressel. op. cit.
22. M.Smilansky. *Besdot uqraina*, n.d. p.113.

ally, he comes under the influence of Tolstoy, and becomes sympathetic to the notion of Socialism, although only of the voluntaristic type.[23] So, he is drawn to the universal models of human and social amelioration, and, specifically, to the perceived needs of his people. These are, for him, located in the resurrection of the ancient homeland, where they will be able to raise their present status, and even be transformed from their lowly status as "Jews" to being the "people of Israel" once more.[24] He also came very much under the influence of Ahad Haam (1856-1927)[25], the great Hebrew editor, publicist and essayist, who argued for a more informed and educated attitude to aliyah. Although business conditions were improving locally, in 1890 a new wave of Palestinian immigration became possible as governmental restrictions there were suddenly relaxed. He is made aware, both through the disappointment suffered by his father in his attempt to emigrate, and by warnings given by those returning from Palestine, that conditions are going to be very tough there. But he had already made his decision, although he could now appreciate more what he was going to lose in a place where there are 'no fields and no gardens, but all depends on us. The land of the ancestors awaits its children, who are to come and make it fruitful, turning it into the paradise that it once was in days of old.'[26] The Jews are to cease being just middlemen and shopkeepers in order to become primary producers and farmers.

So the rest of the story takes place in the Palestine, to which the Ukrainian background, the Diaspora, had served as a prelude. In a way, Smilansky's life reflects the history of Zionism, from its beginnings until well after the establishment of the State, and his writing provides the accompaniment to the action. At the early stage, the young Yehuda is witness to the desperation and to the fallout. He also hears now and sees at first hand something of the major disease that was to plague the scene ever after, the conflict with the Arabs over rights, ownership and territory. But when apprised of this, he argues: 'There is plenty of space here. Over there, it is crowded, in

23. Ibid. p.146.
24. Ibid. p.165.
25. Pen name of Asher Ginzberg.
26. Ibid. p.196.

the Diaspora, where there is nowhere to flee.'[27] This issue, that of drawing the two peoples closer together, was to preoccupy him henceforth, and he was one of the first to write about the local inhabitants, fictionally, in a sustained manner. He strongly opposes any policy of making life so hard for the neighbours that they are driven out.[28] He is fascinated by the Bedouin, and associates them (in his own mind) with the Cossacks, indigenous to the Land. He is fascinated, but he also faces hostility and enmity. The Arabs and Jews are, for him, rival claimants.[29] As he sees it, there are two views in regard to the alternative claims. One is based on historical rights, the second on actual presence. And he adds: 'It seems to me that both views are mistaken. The truth lies somewhere in between. You cannot drive the Arabs out of the country and uproot them from the soil that they are actually tilling. And, likewise, the Jews cannot be told and are not able to find an alternative homeland. One people can not have two homelands.'[30] He adds to the list of his idols the name of Ben-Yehuda, whose activity in Hebrew language revival was seen as a necessary adjunct to the overall national renaissance. But his baptism of fire was to be agricultural work, and he just had to find the appropriate framework. He visits the early colonies, such as Petah Tiqvah and Hadera. Eventually, Yehuda decides, at the age of 18½, after two years in the Land, to purchase a holding in Rehovot. He is now a farmer in a Hebrew colony.

Ahad Haam and his Critique

Smilansky, in his context, was a moderate proponent of Hebrew settlement. He was also to become a strong supporter of the so-called political Zionism propounded by Herzl and his associates. So he believed in the gradualist movement of individuals and groups to Palestine in order to resurrect the soil, and so restore self-respect to the Jewish nation. He also came to support the search for a political

---

27. M.Smilansky. *Baaravah.* n.d. p.36.
28. Ibid. p.47.
29. Ibid. pp.169, 170.
30. Ibid. p.227.

mandate, to be granted by the comity of nations under international law, as it was to be formulated by the World Zionist Organisation, after its establishment in 1897. But both tendencies were challenged and modified, even by their supporters. The first, that of piecemeal settlement, although strongly advocated and applauded by Ahad Haam, was also seen as unruly, undisciplined, and, in the long term, self-defeating. If this tendency, he argued, were to face overwhelming obstacles, it would not only cease to grow, it might disappear altogether, to become a minor footnote in history. In fact, we can see from the testimony of such as Smilansky himself that there were times when it looked as though the total enterprise might totally collapse. The combination of inimical factors, as noted above, could easily prove too much for people unprepared in their task and not fully aware of what lay before and how to act. Ahad Haam then counselled preparation, education and gradualism.

It was not until much later in his life, early in 1922, not long before his death, that Ahad Haam in fact came to settle in Palestine. So when he wrote his first essays, from 1889 onwards, he was speaking only as a sympathiser and a member of the "Lovers of Zion", to which he owed primary allegiance, as an observer and early visitor to Palestine, but not as an immigrant. He was at that stage still resident in the country of his birth, the Ukraine, although he had moved to the great cosmopolitan and Hebrew centre, Odessa, in the Summer of 1886.[31] Odessa, amongst its other connections with Hebrew culture, served as the home of the society of the "Lovers of Zion" Society under the presidency of Leo Pinsker (1821-1891), author of *Autoemanzipation* (1882). It was in 1888 that the editor of *Hamelitz*, on a visit there, hearing of the promising new Hebrew writer, persuaded Ahad Haam to write a piece for his paper. This turned out to be the famous essay "Lo zeh haderekh" (The Wrong Way), which, following delay because of censorship and editorial quirks, appeared in the paper in the Spring of the following year. It dealt with the situation of the new settlement in Palestine and with its backup in the "Lovers of Zion" Movement. But that was only the

---

31. See what is still the best English account of Ahad Haam's life; Leon Simon. *Ahad Ha-am: A Biography.* The Jewish Publication Society of America. Philadelphia, 1960.

starting point, as the author proceeded from there to offer a critique of the current state of Judaism overall. The assumption behind his diagnosis was that there was a malaise in the Movement, as could be evidenced by the lack of dynamism in the growth of the total settlement, the *yishuv*, the dropout rate, the financial bankruptcy, and general lack of vision. But the diagnosis also contained an etiology, and a theoretical, structural analysis relating to the sweep of Jewish history. In Ahad Haam's stated view, the loss of independent nationhood amongst the Jews brought in its trail a loss too of the sense of collective responsibility. As long as there had been an integrated nation, national fulfilment stood as a goal, and underpinned its joint focus. Since the dispersion, each individual acted only for himself. Incidentally, that selfishness is the source, attributed by the author here, of the post-Biblical belief in individual life after death. Hitherto, eternity had been associated with the people as a whole, and there had been no need, in the author's view, for a belief in personal immortality. Now, what was needed was to recover that sense of people hood, that feeling for the collective goal, which had been jettisoned. What had been mistaken in the Zion project hitherto, in the 80s, was precisely the appeal to the individual. The leaders of the Movement, instead of educating its membership in nationhood, in recognition of reality, in historical truth and the knowledge of the sources, for the sake of creating an unselfish and mutually supportive collective, had been appealing instead to personal interest and selfish greed. This order of priorities had to be reversed. The immediate implication for current policy was that the accent should be placed, not on sending as many individuals as quickly as possible to the maximum number of colonies, but rather that a thorough training and background should be secured, so that the project, when carried out, should be well based and long lasting. In the long term, the "Love of Zion" could stand for the whole Jewish scene, and, if properly nurtured in this elitist sense, could herald a genuine revival of Judaism.

Ahad Haam wrote this first essay without having visited Palestine, on the basis of reports and on the basis of his own theoretical constructions. His essay though did make a considerable impact on the Movement and on the life of the settlement. We have already seen that Smilansky did not feel sabotaged or betrayed in his efforts and sacrifice by Ahad Haam's intervention, but rather encouraged, by a critique that he saw as justified and constructive. Although Ahad Haam was judged at the time, and to some extent thereafter, to be negative and carping, he also, even on the basis of such a small body of work, acquired a considerable reputation as scholar, theorist and Hebrew stylist. It was important for the "Love of Zion" Movement to get him to see the Palestinian situation at first hand, and then make further reports and recommendations on the basis of live acquaintanceship with the situation. And so it was that a series of visits was arranged for the budding author. So Ahad Haam first went to Palestine in 1891 for several months, when he visited the colonies, Rishon Lezion, Petah Tiqvah, Rehovot, Gedera and Kastinieh. He published his account and conclusions in a long essay, serialised in instalments in *Hamelitz*, entitled "Emet meeretz yisrael" (Truth from the Land of Israel).[32] He followed this up with a further series of "supplements" to the essay in 1893, in the wake of his second visit there, this time for six weeks only, in May of that year. Although this is not the account of an immigrant, it does derive from that period, relates deliberately to that experience, and thus constitutes a reaction to the contact with the Land. But, characteristically, it also takes the enquiry further, radically posing the question, already formulated more generally in the introduction to the published collection of his writings, as to what may be the overall object of the project. This was whether it might be achievable, and, if so, by what means: 'What is our hope here for the long term? Is the land capable of coming to life once more, and are the Jews capable of bringing it to life?'[33] The author's purpose here, as he says, is neither to sentimentalise nor to soothe, and not to be 'a lyre for songs of Zion' in the vein of that phase of Hebrew poetry known as the "Hibat tziyon" genre, expressing yearning for a distant and unattainable Eden. His purpose is rather to stir the people, to make them aware of the reality. He presents himself, above all, as an iconoclast, as a

---

32. This and the previous essay are included in the first of the four volumes of Ahad Haam's collected essays, *Al parashat drakhim* (At the Crossroads). Jüdischer Verlag. Berlin, 1921.
33. See Ahad Haam. Ibid. vol.1, p.36.

destroyer of myths. Of these, here are some: 1. That there is an infinite supply of land for purchase. In fact, there is very little cultivable land left, and what there is very poor, sandy or stony. 2. That all Arabs are wild Bedouin, unaccustomed to current practice and mores. In fact, the Arabs are very well aware of what is going on, and what our intentions are. 3. That the Ottoman government is weak and feckless. In fact, it is patriotic, and will, in the long run, care for its own interests and religion. In the light of all these illusions and others, if the Jews expect to have a chance of success in purchase, settlement, acclimatisation, large scale immigration, as well as in proper integration into the foreign life of the Orient, then they must take the necessary steps, which, in a word, involve "preparation". And this preparation, in the language of the author, consisted above all in the "preparation of hearts", i.e. in laying the basis psychologically and socially for a successful implementation of a planned programme.

Conclusion

What we have seen here amounts to a collision between fantasy and reality. The Jewish people throughout its history has become accustomed to harking back to a distant past, without the painstaking concomitant effort of integrating that past into the present. Jewish autonomy in Palestine was lost two millennia earlier, and the communities scattered across European and Asian territories. What was held in mind was not so much the reality, as the memory of a reality, perhaps even the memory of a memory. So, to act out on the basis of that mental picture might become shocking in its realisation. When, under the influence of political circumstances and doctrines, with the persecutions and the rise of modern nationalism, the Jews made systematic efforts to return to Zion and then to reconstruct the community through settlement, even before the advent of political Zionism, the way, unsurprisingly, was beset by obstacles. The workers discovered this, and the writers record it. Sometimes, indeed, workers and writers are one and the same, carrying out both functions. It was not only a case of East meeting West, but also of past meeting present, of a clash of cultures, a clash of circumstances. The difficulties might not have proved unsurpassable, but they certainly were, and continue to prove, formidable.

The writers, deriving from a European Enlightenment tradition, Hebrew version, were now attempting the incorporation of late nineteenth century Palestine into the scope of their opus. This Land could be idealised, as the idealisation of Palestine was also established as a literary mode by then. But it was not long before a new and distinctive tone began to replace the earlier approach. This was projected by such a cool thinking realistic observer as Ahad Haam, and it sank into the consciousness and practice of the mainstream writers of the second wave of immigration, from the middle of the first decade of the twentieth century and beyond. The issues then raised and the positions adopted indeed, have been rehearsed ever since. The arguments are continuing in like vein, although they are obviously expressed differently in the light of changed circumstances and fashions.

III

THE ISRAELI NOVEL SINCE 1948

Historical Background

The principal language of the Israeli novel is Hebrew, and Hebrew narrative is as old as the literary language itself. It is inextricably bound up with the text of the Bible, which, in the form which we have, and which has been canonised, opens with stories. There are creation stories, stories of the emergence of mankind, and then extensive family sagas; accounts of the ancestors of the family of man in general, and of the family of the Hebrews in particular. These stories in a sense may be seen as precursors to the Hebrew novel, especially as later Biblical books constitute self-contained narratives, as, for example the Books of *Ruth* and *Esther*. Whether these may regarded as novellas (they are very short) stricto sensu or not remains in dispute. But there is no doubt that from that time on, narrative formed a principal element in the overall stock of Hebrew literary material, sacred or secular.

The normally accepted division of Hebrew literature indeed into sacred and secular may not hold good for the ancient Hebrew world, where it seems that all the known and preserved corpus was regarded as sacred. In order to emphasise a distinction that was perceived later, the notion of the specially sacred text was introduced. Presumably, all other contemporaneous Hebrew literature disappeared, when it was not considered in this category, and thus not particularly worthy of preservation. Later Hebrew literature, that of the Rabinnic period, corresponding roughly to the period beginning with about the first century BC in Palestine and through to the early middle ages, usually took its starting point from the Biblical text, and extended into exegesis and homiletics. But, fanning out from that, stories abounded, sometimes forming literary units, although these were not separated off into separate books, constituting literature for literature's sake. Secular Hebrew literature seemed to re-emerge in the middle ages, to a large extent in competition with Arabic literary forms, after the settlement in Southern Spain from the ninth century onwards. Here we encounter phenomena such as the rhymed story or *maqama* and other literary modes.

The novel per se is a late genre in general world literature. But, in Hebrew literature, it appears even much later. Hebrew literature, after the secular ventures in Spain, and following the Spanish school, to a limited degree in Italy, Holland and other places, turned in on itself, and spoke exclusively of and to the Jewish community, concerning itself with matters of Jewish law, history and the rhythms of Jewish life. It opened itself up once more to outside influences under the pressure of Emancipation and Enlightenment. Movements originating in eighteenth century Germany sought to reintroduce the Jews into the cultural world of Europe, and created a literature to promote this cause. But, even within this context, the novel is a latecomer. Not until the early nineteenth century do we have anything that looks like a genuine novel written in Hebrew. The first attempts at Hebrew novel writing in the modern sense were epistolary satires of Hasidic life and mores, composed in Galicia. Some even advance the notion of the origins of the Hebrew novel to mid nineteenth century Vilna, with the creation of pseudo Biblical romance by Avraham Mapu, deploying solely Biblical language in his first narrative, *Ahavat tsiyon* (1851, Love of Zion). Fighting the constraints of this formula, but still operating within Eastern Europe, later writers towards the end of the century expanded the means, using Hebrew from all periods and also imitating Yiddish models (including their own works) to move into the mode that particularly sets the "novel" aside as a self-contrained genre, i.e. the realistic comment on current life as would be recognised by the reader. Yiddish was overwhelmingly the vernacular employed by the Jews within the Pale of Settlement, whereas the use of Hebrew was confined to liturgical and certain limited literary contexts. The modern Hebraists sought to rectify this, and to introduce the general use of Hebrew as a language of total register, particularly secular literature. This phase happened to coincide historically with the rise of the Zionist Movement (from the 1890s and specifically 1897, the first Zionist Congress) and the beginnings of the Return to Palestine on the part of the Jews, within a modern and even political framework. A major part of this Zionising program was the inculcation and everyday use of the Hebrew language, as well as the propagation of a large scale literature, on the European model, in all genres. This was the tradition to which the Israeli phase is heir.

Since Israel was only declared an independent State in 1948, any literature produced before that date is technically non Israeli. In practice, however, May 1948 does not constitute a particularly significant literary watershed. The principal official language of the new State was to be Hebrew, and, as we have seen, Israeli literature inherited the long tradition of Hebrew literature, whose origins are biblical and whose written output extended over several millennia and to all those parts of the world where Jewish communities and culture flourished. Hebrew had already been recognised as an official language within mandatory Palestine.

More specifically, Israeli literature follows the tradition of the new Hebrew literature, encapsulating two major trends: (1) the secularising, although partially national, tendency of the Jewish Enlightenment and (2) the nationalistic tendency towards a return to the ancient Palestinian homeland, where the reborn culture might flourish unhampered. The Hebrew Enlightenment struggled for increased lexical and syntactic scope, and for an extension of literary genres beyond medieval and traditional bounds. A breakdown of old forms of community and religious practice in the wake of secularisation and social unrest was noted by the greatest of the Hebrew masters, sometimes with enthusiasm and sometimes with foreboding. In the late nineteenth century, satirists such as the Yiddish and Hebrew novelist, Shalom Yaakov Abromowitz, better known by his pen name, Mendele Mokher Sforim (1836-1917), both attacked social patterns and mourned the passing of the old. The

57

leading poet of the generation, who also wrote stories and other prose works, Chayim Nachman Bialik (1873-1934), blended his own sense of existential tragedy with a description of the unique character of the Jewish people to create the effect of an ineradicable pathos.

Until World War 1, the chief centres of modern Hebrew creativity remained in the Diaspora, particularly in Eastern Europe. But the ravages of that war, the Bolshevik revolution, and the Russian civil war effectively destroyed the old style Pale of Settlement and the *shtetl* within. It was the existence of a largely autonomous Jewish society that facilitated the production of specifically Jewish literature, mainly in Hebrew and Yiddish. This process of decline was to be completed by the Holocaust of European Jewry. But already, the victory in the Great War of the British, who had offered the Balfour Declaration of November 1917, stimulated the movement of Jews to Palestine. This wave of Jewish emigration to the Holy Land, (now the third such wave) of the period following the war more than doubled the existing Jewish settlement, and, in spite of major setbacks, the so-called *yishuv* (Jewish community of Palestine) established itself as a State in the making (State on the Way, as it is known in the Hebrew nomenclature). The ongoing disaster of European Jewry reinforced this tendency, so that by 1939, an independent political entity, a State, now challenged by systematic Arab opposition, could begin to emerge. Other centres of Hebrew creativity were dying in three major areas: (1) in Western Europe, where the Holocaust was to trap the Jews, and, of course, their culture; (2) in Eastern Europe, where Communism was throttling the "counter revolutionary" language of Hebrew, together with other independent sources of Jewish expression; and (3) in the USA (which had become the home of the single largest Jewish population in the world), where cultural and linguistic assimilation was proceeding apace. In the new circumstances, only Palestine/Israel constituted a possible Hebrew centre.

Israel

With Israeli independence in 1948, Hebrew could flourish not just as a literary language but as a current vernacular and the mainstream medium of expression in the new State. But already, Hebrew writers of the early part of the century had established themselves in Palestine, so that by the 1920s a self-conscious Palestinian-Hebrew literature had been created. Avraham Shlonsky (1900-1973), Uri Zvi Greenberg (1896-1983) and Natan Alterman (1910-1970), all poets nourished in Eastern Europe, moved to Palestine during this period with the third wave. The person who may perhaps be regarded as the greatest of all Hebrew novelists and short story writers, S.Y. Agnon (1888-1970), returned to Palestine from Germany in 1924 after an earlier stay there before World War 1. The Oriental Hebrew novelist Yehuda Burla (1887-1969) was Palestinian born, as was the poetess Esther Raab (1899-1981). On the one hand, there existed an inherent relationship to the local soil on the part of the native writer, and, on the other, some of the immigrant writers, in various ways, sought to assume a Palestinian identity by obliterating traces of the Diaspora. The earlier warnings issued by Yosef H. Brenner (1881-1921) against the deployment of the Palestinian genre as such might have exerted their influence on the writers of the second wave of immigration, from circa 1909 onwards, but this third wave (1919-1924) saw Palestine and a specifically local literature established as a major focus. In *Masada* (1924), a long poem by Yitzhak Lamdan (1900-1954), the poetic narrator idealizes labour in the tones appropriate to a Russian revolutionary poet; U.Z. Greenberg dons prophetic garb in his ultra nationalistic, fiery verse; Agnon turns to the Palestinian epic, in addition to his large scale threnodies of the old, East European Jewish settlement; and Chayim Hazaz (1898-1972), another notable novelist, incorporates the Palestinian scene in his narrative subject matter. The Palestinian genre was becoming just as much an accepted norm as the narrative recall of the virtually extinct communities of Europe.

So, by 1948, the literary mode of the national literature was already established, just as the social and political moulds had also settled. Inevitably, some of the most notable and typical exponents of

Israeli literature had begun writing earlier. The Palestinian born novelist S.Yizhar (Smilansky) (b.1916) began to publish in 1938, seeking a richer lexical and syntactic language for the expressive consciousness of his narrative pivot. However long his story, his plot is always sparse. His central concerns are the landscape, for which he tried in his virtuosic deployment of the deepest and most obscure layers of the Hebrew language, the moral issue (presented in terms of selection of one option from two opposites), the indecisive hero, and the texture of the Hebrew language, the quintessential instrument of a language that had to be revived as an essential tool for the creation of a vibrant and contemporary literature. But the movement of the narrative remains characteristically unresolved by any decisive action, and no change takes place. Between the mid 1960s and throughout the 70s and the 80s, Yizhar wrote almost no fiction. But, in the early 90s, he began to produce fiction once more, hitherto four full length books, again ploughing the memories of childhood, the self identity of the developing youth in mandatory Palestine and the overwhelming power of the landcape. Now, he is more willing to tackle subjects that perhaps seemed too sensitive at the time; the issue of women for example, and emotional involvement on the part of the male protagonist/s. He, like so many other writers of his generation, had practically eschewed feminine subjects, and those touching on sexuality, except of the most general and blandest nature.[1] The poetry and prose of Haim Gouri (b.1923), which started to appear at the close of the War of Independence, focuses on war, the hero, his beloved, and his bloody memories - a very local scene. Many of the heroes in the novels and stories of Moshe Shamir (b.1921) are not only native born, but see themselves as a different species from the Diaspora Jew. The Israeli (the new Hebrew) is characterized as simple, direct, active, healthy, single-minded and strong, in contrast to the split, urban, tortured Diaspora Jew. Shamir,

---

1. In a representative selection of this writing, made ahortly after the War of Independence, *Qeshet sofrim*, Tel Aviv, Spring 1949, out of seventeen participants, there is only one woman writer (Yehudit Hendel). See Nurit Guvrin, "Adam bamilhamah" in ed. Mordechai Naor, *Qesher*. Tel Aviv, May 1998. The subjects adopted by the writers, naturally enough, reflect the war situation in all its forms, and are overwhelmingly "masculine".

like many others who sought to make a literary and ideological mark, set up a small journal, *Yalqut hareim,* and the general description of this writing as "Palmach literature" (named after the striking arm of the *Haganah* - Defense Force) owes its origins to this sense of comradeship and a single, collective purpose. The subject matter for treatment was, in general, emergent Israel: absorption of immigrants, the war, the kibbutz, the issues of the new State. The concerns were practical and ideological, of public polity rather than of the individual.

The 1950s witnessed changes on various fronts. Poets became more introspective and sceptical, doubtful of the collective thrust, and began uncertainly to look back to their forbears and to earlier Jewish existence. Yehuda Amichai (b.1924), in poetry and in prose, made much of the contrast between the generations, highlighted by the surprising image become metaphor. Pinhas Sadeh (1929-1994), seeing "life as a parable" (the title of his magnum opus, 1958), started to produce a rather "un-Israeli" type of confessional prose, whose concerns were the self, truth and God. Intense religious experience has not been a prominent theme of Israeli authors, although the poetess Zelda (1914-1984), fairly late in life, began to express an ecstatic certainty of God's presence in the unremitting face of death. But away from public commitments, the heroes of Israeli novels of the 1950s and 1960s are seen in flight from their official or their imagined roles. Shamir's work also moved in this direction. The characters of the novelist Aharon Megged (b.1920) are sometimes disillusioned, making their way from the kibbutz to the city, as in *Hedvah vaani* (1954; Hedva and I) or away from the sense of subjugation to the national myth, as in *Hachai al hamet* (1965; The living on the dead).[2]

Israeli existence was, of course, multifaceted. But ideologies had not only been promoted for the purposes of engagement in conflict, when ideological positioning might have been regarded as existential necessity, but sometimes as something peculiar and exclusive to the new Israel. One such ideology was aired in the

---

2. This theme is treated in Leon Yudkin, *Escape into Siege.* Routledge and Kegan Paul. London, 1974, pp. 90-115.

periodical *Alef*, which was founded in the 1940s to advocate a sort of Hebrew Semitic Union unconnected with Diaspora Jewry, and which continued to press for a secular Middle Eastern State. It was perceived that Israel had to establish its own separate identity as a precondition for the finding of an individual voice. Another, although less dogmatic, ideology was crystallised in a journal entitled *Liqrat*, distributed from 1952 onwards, and which adopted neither a leftist nor a rightist orientation, seeking a moderate, temperate and humane direction. These were alternative voices to the predominant thrust of public policy as expressed in the new Israel, i.e. the thrust of militant Zionism. But these alternative voices were often muted, as the literature of the State of Israel in general became less sure of itself and its direction less certain. Israel was and is characterised by division, and has become increasingly "normalized", that is, its people are now more concerned with their own personal situation. So too has its literature become less publicly orientated, although the Land of Israel, (Eretz Yisrael), naturally remains, at least subliminally, its subject. It is its object too, in the sense that the literature expresses ideological aspirations for the country.

More recent years have seen projections backwards in time, to earlier history formative of the present, and forwards, to a concern with total contemporaneity. Aharon Appelfeld (b.1932), in fiction such as *Badenheim ir nofesh* (1975; *Badenheim 1939*, 1980), writes mainly of Israel's prehistory, of a European Jewry in its twilight world, reaching for assimilation on its path to destruction, and of the world of the survivors in Israel rooted in that past. It is both the world of the author's childhood and the public Israeli world of an often unacknowledged infancy. The novelist A.B. Yehoshua, (b.1937), author of *Bithilat qayits 1970* (1971; *Early in the Summer of 1970, 1977)* and *Hameahev* (1977; *The Lover,* 1978), amongst others, has stated that his purpose is to render Israeli man and his paradoxical dilemmas. Amos Oz (b.1939) has sought symbols for the Israeli situation, images of terror and siege that haunt ordinary people whose interior lives are really quite extraordinary. He too has attempted to recover his own childhood world and the pre-1948 Palestinian world in a collection of novellas with the overall title of *Har haetsah haraah* (1976; *The Hill of Evil Counsel,* 1978. A more recent novel,

Panther bamartef, 1995; (Panther in the Basement), returns to the creation of the atmosphere of the last days of the British Mandate in Palestine as perceived by a child of the *yishuv.*

The current scene abounds with experimentation in mimesis. Amalia Kahana-Carmon (b.1926) has long been writing intensely rendered stream of consciousness fiction, often as though narrated by a child or by an adult with a childlike vision, fixated on another individual. Yaakov Shabtai (1934-1981) produced a series of short narrative extravaganzas, then a long novel of a single paragraph, *Zikhron dvarim* (1977; *Past Continuous*, 1985), moving from one death at its opening to another at its close, the first that of Goldmann's father, the second the suicide of his son. It moves as well from the banal to the tragic with apparently effortless control. His posthumous novel, *Sof davar* (1984; *Past Perfect*, 1987) was issued unedited by the author, following his very early death, and follows the line of associative narrative, this time experimenting with different modes and time scales.[3]

Confessional autobiography of the type cast by Sadeh, although without Sadeh's religious mysticism but with a fair admixture of humor, has been produced by Dan Ben-Amots (1923-1994), either directly, reporting his own history, or through some other guise, thinly veiling the authorial persona. A striking achievement of Israeli fiction is a reconstruction of the European background transmitted, as it were, by a Berlin born narrator, is the novel by David Schutz (b.1941), *Haesev vehahol* (1978; the grass and the sand). Although the narrator Emmanuel controls the novel, different voices are heard within, presenting their account of events and family. It is Emmanuel whose initiative it is to return "home" and attempt a resolution of his past with his present, of himself with his family and background, with a consecutive history going back to mid-Europe of the turn of the century. Late novels of this Berlin born author continue to investigate the complex web of interrelations in Israeli family complexes.

---

3. I have dealt with Shabtai more fully in Leon Yudkin, *Beyond Sequence: Current Israeli Fiction and its Context.* Symposium Press. London, 1992, pp. 45-62.

The Decade of the 80s

In the 80s, it was fiction that proved most adventurous and innovative amongst the genres in Israeli Hebrew literature. The range and
variety of expressive typology indicate some impatience with traditional linear narrative, time bound, place bound, limited to the
traditional restraints of Hebrew grammar and vocabulary. So
narrative was tensed and stretched, mixing modes and forms.
Chronological points were juxtaposed, voices transposed, points of
view shuffled, time sequences broken, narrative segments highlighted
or challenged by alternative versions and statements. All these moves
come to the service of a hoped for greater penetration of the truth of
the narrative.

Leading experimenters have included established authors. Amos
Oz has investigated various methods of handling plot development.
In *Qufsah shehorah* (1987; *Black Box*, 1988), he presents a story
from different viewpoints, through an epistolatory novel. This form,
of its nature, extracts disparate views of the same objective materials;
it is compelled to be heterodiegetic, as there are several tellers. That
is the point of the story. In a later novel, *Ladaat ishah*, (1989, *To
Know a Woman*, 1991), we have a principal narrative consciousness
in the novel's hero, but the different time scales allow another
perspective, as well as some scepticism in regard to the author's own
account. A.B. Yehoshua (b.1936) has continued to experiment with
narrative technique, particularly in *Mar maniy* (1990; *Mr. Mani*,
1992), where the "telephone" mode is adopted. When we hear
someone speaking on the telephone, we not only hear just one side of
what is presumed to be a dialogue, we also inevitably construct the
other side, the dumb side, in our mind. A further technical surprise in
the novel lies in its reversal of conventional expectations. We expect
time to move forward, and fiction often explores results and
implications in the seeds of earlier action. Human experience of time
is progressive, although memory moves back. But *Mr. Mani*, in a
series of five episodes, opens with the most recent, set in the 80s, and
then moves backwards over two centuries in an apparent attempt to
explore the Mani line's place in history. So Yehoshua has played
with various approaches to narrative, including fantasy, surprise,

reversal, stream of consciousness, as well as with the traditional type of narrative (telling a story straight in *Molkho* (1987; *Five Seasons*, 1991). The reader is involved in the understanding and even in the creation of the narrative. In a further deviation from the earlier lines of his fiction, he has written a historical novel, based on the travels of a Rabbi in Europe at the end of the previous millennium, 999, *masa el tom haelef* (1996; Journey to the End of the Millennium).

Fundamental to recent developments has been the contribution of Yaakov Shabtai. His two novels, because of their artistic success, have suggested new ways of representing reality in fiction. The earlier novel is a string of consciousnesses presented from the outside, where time and association link motifs and narrative parts together. Here, time moves on, and the reader has all sorts of markers to facilitate the understanding of the plot. So externality bears closely on internal awareness and does much to engender it. On the other hand, the specific shape of the text is created by the individual consciousness, so that there is constant interplay between the inner and outer layers of reality. Although the story is relayed by the protagonists and seen through their various lenses, the novel as a whole bears the stamp of a unity of vision. Perhaps, this is due to the way that the lives of three protagonists intertwine, particularly during the course of the nine months covered and within the delimited environment of Tel Aviv. The detailed observation, the linguistic precision, the mental associations, the humour and the imagination have created a unitary text. However, Shabtai's posthumous novel, in the main, adopts a quite different approach. Here, there is a single focus of consciousness, holding various approaches the single hero's mental state at an especially critical phase in his life. Reality and fantasy, waking and dream world, are moulded together, as eventually are present and past. The reader is unsure whether objective reality is being presented, or whether it is an alternative version of that reality, with a cocktail of memory and fancy added.

It is these flexible versions of reality which have done something to shift the vistas of recent Israeli fiction. One of the leading voices of the 80s, David Grossman (b.1954), is much concerned with alternative versions of reality, not just within any one particular work, but in the course of his ongoing opus. We can see

Hiyukh hagdiy (1983; *Smile of the Lamb*, 1991) and *Hazman hatsahov* (1987; *Yellow Wind*, 1987) as obverse and reverse sides of a single coin. Both works purport to describe the situation under Israeli occupation in the West Bank and the course of the intifada. But whereas the earlier work is a novel, with a complex view of character, time, motivation and development (imposing considerable strains on the reader), the latter account is journalistic and polemical, tendentious in its straightforward attempt to persuade the reader of a certain understanding of events. Of course, these works represent different genres. But even so, the genres themselves are deliberately jumbled; there is, for example, a story inserted *Yellow Wind*. Grossman's later novel, *Ayen erekh ahavah* (1986; *See Under Love*, 1988), constitutes a very ambitious effort to see the Holocaust afresh, this time through the eyes of a child (the primary account), but also with a variety of narrative devices, including surrealism, fantasy and dictionary definition, all deviating from the linear narrative set up in the primary account. In later work, Grossman has pursued the two tracks of the investigative probing of Jewish-Arab relations (as in *Nokhahim nifqadim*, 1992; *Sleeping on a Wire*, 1993) and that of fictional recreation of childhood (as in *Sefer hadiqduq hapnimiy*, 1991; *The Book of Intimate Grammar*, 1994).

Other novelists who are interested in expanding fictional range through magic realism include Itamar Levy (b.1956). Magic realism is on the one hand anchored to reality and seeks to explore it, but, on the other, it handles it freely and so can dispense with the laws of fictional gravity. In the case of fiction, the limiting determinants are time sequence and limitation of locus. If time sequences can be shifted, speeded up or slowed down (as has been done in all fiction through the ages), skipped and reversed, if distances can be contracted and places moved, and if the narrative voice can allow itself the freedom to shift in and out of various characters at will and at need, then a kaleidoscope of effects can be achieved. Magic realism is the product of a growing need to absorb larger and more astonishing segments of actuality, to confront the incredible with the surprising, and to provide innovative tools in the search for accurate and illuminating representation.

The Current Scene

Fiction has moved in all sorts of diverse directions, and Israeli fiction is likewise experimental. We have seen that Yehoshua has allowed the reader space in which to create the missing parts of the dialogue in his "telephone" novel. Y. Hoffman (b.1937) has his novels printed only on one side of the leaf, so that the reader is confronted by a blank page for every printed page. Is the reader to create his own story, his own counterpoint? He has indeed no alternative but to do this. Yuval Shimoni (b.1955), in *Meof hayonah* (1990; the flight of the dove), writes two parallel stories on facing pages in different print types, and these stories intersect in time and place. One is the story of an American couple visiting Paris as tourists, and the second is of a lonely woman living there. But, in other fictional experiments, plot may be abandoned completely, as by Aner Shalev in *Opus 1* (1988), where, as the title implies, narrative, as in Pater's motto, aspires to the condition of music. Instead of the normal components of narrative, such as linear time, logical sequence, coherent plot, we have a sort of musical notation - staccato, legato etc. Or we have, as in the novel by Avraham Heffner (b.1935), *Sefer hamforash* (1991; explicated book), a work with its own commentary attached to the text. In this particular case, the reader is not left alone to draw his conclusions, but is bombarded with suggestions, options and interpretations.

But, of course, literature is not music. It is made of words, and words have meanings, connotations and implications for external reality. One line of experimentation in fiction can lead to its own demise or silence. Fiction, i.e. invention, can create prodigiously, not only materials, but also ways of looking at materials. Frustration is inevitable in the search for the nugget of truth that is thought to lie at the source, or for the catchall means of grasping that truth. Reality is enormous, and it is the function of the writer to sharpen its outlines and encapsulate it. As reality expands in our consciousness and we learn more, so literature has to expand its capacity. This, at any rate, seems to be the impulse behind the ambition.

Nevertheless, literary concerns, in that they are human, remain stable, and our consciousness, together with the means adopted for its representation, limited. We want to know how people understand each other, how they see themselves and others, and how they interpret their mutual interaction. One of the most notable features of recent Israeli literature is the increased articulacy of the female writer, a dynamic presence in the world and on the page. Amalia Kahana-Carmon has long given expression to a specifically feminine view of interpersonal contact. But now, many others, in prose and poetry, are presenting a more proactive view of the world, entering a domain hitherto held to be an exclusively male preserve, initiating relationships, reinvesting sexual imagery with the vocabulary of female need, and generally placing the woman (often the I of the narrative) in the forefront of the fiction. Together with the transformed view of the world, there is heard a new tone in the fiction, humorous, slangy and irreverent. Of such character are the surrealistic forays of Orly Castel-Bloom (b.1960), the slangy and challenging naturalism of Irit Linur (b.1958) and the demotic humor of Yehudit Katzir (b.1963). A collection of Katzir's novellas appeared in 1970, *Sogrim et hayam* (1990; Closing the Sea), and was immediately successful, appealing to a reading public, thirsty for a lowering of the severe literary tone predominant, presented with deft wit. Linur's three novels, *Shirat hasirena* (1991; The Siren's Song), *Shtey shilgiyot* (1993; Two Snow-Whites) and *Hasandlarit* (1997; Sandler Ella) are first person full length narratives, in which the author dons an effective disguise. She uses a conversational argot, building up a credible, exciting narrative of everyday life in Tel-Aviv. The first work is set at the time of the Gulf War, with the threat of Scud missiles hanging over the city. Paradoxically, the second, already far removed from the immediate concerns of the first, is of a more sombre character. What is admirable and innovative is the manner in which an apparently facile language is deployed with utmost plasticity to serve as an alternative literary mode. The narrative posture is amusing but not forced or strained. This feminism is sexy rather than sexist, relishing the delights of the flesh and expressing the anguish of the concomitant frustrations. The woman here is an initiator, but still, above all, interested in men, without being subservient. The private passions are operative in the public sphere. There is no doubt that the massive intervention of the woman writer in Israeli fiction within the last decade or so has introduced a new dimension into the narrative. Now, the personal theme predominates rather than the social, public, philosophical or political. And whereas hitherto, the plaint has frequently been voiced that Hebrew literature lacks humor, female fiction here is usually witty and underplayed. The Linur heroine, for example, does not take herself too seriously, and an admirable distance is preserved between the narrative voice and the person of the author. This is a quality that has been notably absent in other sorts of confessional or first person narrative. In her third novel, she continues to plough this field, still writing in the first person, narrating an apparently highly successful television personality. The most successful element of this narrative is the amusing and self deprecating throw away humour. The less successful aspect is the inability to develop character and plot, in favour of a somewhat arbitrary development. The heroine moves from one job to another, as she does from one lover to another, never fully engaging the reader in her motivation and shifts. We, like herself, do not understand why she marries the feckless and dominating Pe'er, anymore than why she chooses to keep this marriage a secret, to the perplexity of everyone else and the inconvenience of herself. Things seem to happen, just because they do, arbitrarily, not through any internal necessity, character development or narrative motor. This can have the dangerous effect of producing a somewhat wearisome and repetitive story line, extended for its own sake, and then ending abruptly. The novel here does indeed end in a fairy tale manner, allowing us all to be content with the happy ever after situation of her eventual union with her third lover, Tsahi. Tendencies of utilitarian fiction in Israel, seeking out the greatest happiness of the greatest number, can be taken too far.

But there are other tendencies as well. Yitzhak Laor (b.1948) pursues a line of political protest in his multi-generic efforts in fiction, poetry and drama. Aharon Appelfeld , in his later work too, still situates his stories in a tragic European past, with the fictional characters seeking to flee their destiny or to avoid its recognition. A very complex picture emerges in any survey of the Israeli fictional scene. Certainly, as for some time now, the dominant language is

Hebrew, although literature in other languages is being produced by, for example, English speaking expatriates, by more recent Soviet immigrants, or by Arabs, challenging Hebrew and Jewish hegemony in the Land. A Hebrew literary tradition has been inherited and modified, sometimes by writers with little knowledge of or sympathy for that tradition. Hebrew is a language rich in traditional and liturgical associations but young as a vernacular. Its writers are of several generations and vastly disparate cultural and geographical backgrounds. But they jostle together in the turbulent currents of Hebrew literature: the young and the old, the Israeli-born and the recent immigrant, the Zionist conservative and the radical, the Oriental and the European Jew, the Hebrew writing Arab, the religious and the secular Jew, the hopeful and the disillusioned.

Public sphere, private sphere

One of the characteristics of the current situation in literature and culture generally is the degree to which the separation of the categories has become problematic, if not untenable. The public sphere is constantly impinging on the private. The converse also holds true, as each domain seems to break its own boundaries and stray on to the territory of the other. In Israel, the murder of prime minister, Yitzhak Rabin, who signed the peace accord with Yasser Arafat, in the view of some commentators on the scene, not only merged the two spheres, but also blurred the distinction between the meaningful and the meaningless.[4] Gadi Taub, in his analysis of the current atmosphere of Israeli culture, argues that the reduction of significance has created a nostalgia for the large public moment, as in the collection of short stories by Etgar Kerrett.[5] A confusion is created between the large event and the trivial response, the public and the private. In his story, "Balata",[6] the little hero can move on to

---

4. For a discussion of this issue see Gadi Taub, *Hamered hashafuf* (The Dispirited Rebellion). Hakibbutz hameuhad. Tel Aviv, 1997, specifically p. 18 and c.
5. Etgar Kerrett, *Gaaguay lekisinger* (My Longings for Kissinger). Zmorah Bitan. Tel Aviv, 1994.
6. In Etgar Kerrett, *Tsinorot* (Pipelines). Am Oved. Tel Aviv, 1992.

the border of greatness just by standing on a loose paving stone. There, but only there, can he achieve '[t]he sensation of enchantment that can never be replicated.' In another of his stories, from that same volume (his first published), "Yordan",[7] the narrator creates a double take of a spy story. He becomes his own suspect, whilst working for the Israeli secret service, and comes to the reluctant conclusion that '[d]eep down inside himself, he still did not trust him', i.e. referring back to himself. The use of the mirror creates a metaphor to suggest a split identity, looking both in and out, seeing himself from both angles. And there remains a residue of profound scepticism.

The creation of a meaningful avant garde, says Taub,[8] is contingent on consensus, which the new, rebellious tendency breaches. Such consensus acts as a bench mark, a line of acceptability. But now, there is no consensus. All is permitted, and everything exists on the same plain of equal banality. This is of course a phenomenon that is observable well beyond Israel, and may hold good, to some extent, throughout the world. The function of the avant garde is both to shock, and to invite the audience to see the presented artefact, and indeed the history of the artistic tradition to which that presentation belongs, in a new light. But this can only work if the tradition that is being challenged is respected, and associated with a scale of shared values. If there is no value scale accepted, then there can be no challenge, as the wall would already have been breached, and the ramparts captured. You cannot applaud the undermining of a position which is no longer held.

Much of Israel's fictional vanguard reflects this general mood. Not only do we rush from one event to another, we also move from one sensation to another, and that very quickly, without dwelling too long on any one situation. In the contemporary film, scenes of violence replace each other with bewildering rapidity. In the television soap, disparate plots are heaped up one on top of another, and then interrupted by snatches of advertisement for disparate products. The viewer/reader is not allowed to get bored, and to ensure that, he is also not permitted to stay very long with any single

7. Ibid.
8. Taub, ibid, the argument is presented in the whole first section.

subject. Murders are succeeded by rapes, robberies, feasts or ennui. Fiction captures and renders this flickering parade. "Shards" and "fugitive pieces" are not only the necessary residue of unspeakable trauma, but the common property of verbal representation of current reality. Once again, literature has to find the appropriate means to render the current mood; the novel still has to be new. But still, literature has to adhere to the now hallowed tradition that in order to be artistic and relevant, it must needs be rebellious.[9] Art means radicalism and liberation from the chains of the oppressive past and its reactionary tradition.

One of the consequences of this article of faith is that Art is driven further and more frantically in search both of the new statement, but, also, for new ways of formulating the statement. It must never allow the receiver to feel that he has mastered the method, and thus sink into apparent complacency. Assumptions about human personality must be challenged, as must our notion of social arrangements. We must rethink our idea of what constitutes an ending, or indeed a proper beginning or appropriate plot development. We must be challenged in our notions of what belongs where, and in what circumstances. All contents are shaken up, and then inspected anew. The trouble may be however, that when this inspection is carried out, there is nothing against which to measure the product or the criticism. Protest has no impetus within an emotional, aesthetic and ethical vacuum, as it then becomes inoperative, assuming the vacancy of its situated context. Once again, we see that literature must be related to life and take its bearings from the world from which it derives. If the world is trivial, the ironic comment becomes random, and literature itself is then reduced to a cipher.

It seems that there, in respect of our present concern, there are two modes operative in Israeli literature. One, the more prominent, is the system of public and national address; the sense of literature as herald, bearing a message to the Jewish people, the direct and primary addressee. The second mode is the treatment of literature as the receptacle for individual concerns, with the act of writing as the inscription of the mind of the writer, the vehicle for his mental life

---

9. Ibid. p.81.

and all that pertains to it. The first is the more prominent because that is what is specific to the tradition of Hebrew literature. This literature has so notably, even sometimes exclusively, been seen as an ideological tool, the expression of a public message, relating the divine word to the immediate situation. The characteristic mode of Biblical times was indeed prophecy, and the prophetic message was the word of the Lord. Even when that specific charge was reduced, as in the Rabbinic and medieval periods, or secularised, as in the post Enlightenment phase, Hebrew literature was still regarded as possessing a public function of import to the people of "Israel" (Israel in the traditional sense, as used in Bible and traditional sources). Even in modern times, and in the new Palestinian and Israeli phases, we see the Israeli writer very often assuming a very public persona, considering the state of the Nation and its public policy in the light of the changing scene. The alternative mode, the private voice, is the one assumed adopted by all writers, wherever they may be, in whatever tongue or circumstance.

Indeed, we can still recognise this divide. Israel's well known writers, in poetry and prose, may address the nation, and consider its directions, offering analysis, advice or directives. Few are the novels of Amos Oz, for example, which do not have a public bearing and weighty implication. Of course, his fictions differ from his overtly political works, allowing for divergence of views and eccentricity of expression. We should certainly in no wise confuse the voice of any fictional character or narrator with the author's own, which may be disguised, experimental or absent. But the public address is there. And so it is in the writings of A.B. Yehoshua, David Grossman, and even, more obliquely, with Appelfeld. We confront some grasp of the state of the nation, as it was, as it is, or as it could be. There exists the direct transmutation of the political, public concern into the literary expression. This literary expression does of course allow for greater subtlety of tone, shades of stress, variations of pitch, change of mood and stance, the weaving of the individual into the public sphere over the direct, unalloyed political statement. But this literature still does bear traces of the original prophetic stance specific to the Hebrew work.

Not so, or at the least, not so obviously, with the alternative voice. This is the voice of such as Gnessin, Vogel, Kahana Carmon, Sadeh, and increasingly so, of many increasingly prominent women writers. Female writers particularly dwell on other, less public regions. Here, the personal life is central to the narrative, the life of the emotions, passions, interpersonal relations and personal growth. There is also a growing tendency on the part of some writers, such as Aner Shalev and Yuval Shimoni, to situate their narratives in a world stripped of the specific contours of Israel or any residue of overt national consciousness. This is the secondary tendency of Israeli fiction, but a tendency that is becoming increasingly prominent, and may be another epiphenomenon of that country's "normality". We certainly would not wish to adopt any value scale in an overall estimation of the scene, but it is important to note a new balance. This does not mean that the public crisis no longer has its echo in this type of literature, but rather that the manner of its transmutation can be of a different kind.

IV

EDMOND FLEG AND THE JEWISH QUESTION

Background

Edmond Fleg (1874-1963) was born in Geneva in the very year that Switzerland received a new constitution guaranteeing all its citizens freedom of religion and expression. Hitherto, under the 1848 constitution, that facility had been restricted to Christians. Edmond's father, Alsatian in origin, had become naturalised in 1871. As can be seen clearly from his prolific correspondence,[1] he was extremely attached to his parents, particularly to his mother, and retails fond memories of his background and of the Jewish practice which constituted such an essential and inextricable part of his early life. However, according to his autobiographical account in *Pourquoi je suis juif*,[2] Edmond rejected what, at an early stage, he had come to regard as automatic and unthinking ritualism, in search of a universal truth.

He was a brilliant student, and his talents and ambition led him to study in Paris in 1892, where he basically lived for the rest of his life. He was particularly drawn to the "new thinking", and he studied Philosophy and German in pursuit of some mastery of current trends in theoretical concerns. At this early stage, he thought of himself as

---

1. Much of this correspondence is housed in the extremely useful archive at the Alliance Israélite Building in Paris, where much material is on microfiche. I am very grateful to the curators for their generous assistance and access to this material.
2. First published in 1928, and reprinted in 1995.

belonging to the generality of mankind rather than to a specific cult or branch of any particular faith. His proclivities led him into the company of aesthetes, and his early writing, his plays and his poetry, reflect his interest in the current literary, artistic and theatrical movements of the day. He was also much taken by the aesthetic and mythical power of Christianity, although more specifically, by the figure of Jesus, and this attraction held him throughout his life. When his interest in Judaism was reawakened, and, in fact, became an all consuming passion, he became concerned with the possibility of uniting (reuniting?) the two faiths. He focused on the concept of the Messiah. The central difference between Judaism and Christianity was, he argued, that, for the former, the Messiah was an expectation, whereas, for the latter, he had already come, and would surely come again. This was a contradiction that might be happily resolved, and the germ of this possibility he located in various points of history, for example, in the enigmatic figure of Salomon Molco[3] (1500-1532), who befriended the Pope, Clement VII, and to which subject he devoted a play, *Le Juif du Pape*.[4]

But that was far in the future. What was to become one of the most significant events in his life, although it was a very public one that was to affect the whole of French society was the Dreyfus Affair. This broke on the public on November 11 1894, when Alfred Dreyfus was arrested for high treason, on the basis of supposed evidence of a "bordereau" (a slip of paper) assumed to be in Dreyfus's handwriting, giving away military secrets to the Germans. He was found guilty in the following month. On January 5 of the next year, Dreyfus suffered public humiliation, "degradation militaire". At that time, Theodor Herzl was reporting on the Affair for the Viennese paper, the *Neue Freie Presse*. The waves of the Affair were to consume France and the Jewish world for years to come, and the secondary implications were enormous. Herzl attributed his own conversion to the notion of founding a Jewish State to these events, and French Jews, including those who had regarded themselves as assimilated painlessly into the French body politic, were required, or,

---

3. I am following the orthography adopted by Fleg in his play about this figure.
4. First performed between January and March, 1924, Villeflix, and published the following year.

at least, sought, to reassess their position and take stock. It was not so much the fact of the arrest itself, albeit that was, as was manifest later, executed on the basis of exceedingly flimsy, even contradictory evidence. The specific ingredient in this trial and its reception was the evident anti-Semitism behind the charge, and the violent anti-Jewish reaction, disproportionate and uncontrolled, that was evoked in the general public. It was at this point that Fleg too reappraised his position.

In 1896, Fleg's father died.[5] Fleg continued to live in Paris, where he was well integrated into the intellectual life. But he was increasingly pulled by two contrasting intellectual and spiritual tendencies. One was the growing, conservative, romantic patriotism as presented by his friend and colleague, Lucien Moreau, who was now an active anti-Dreyfusard. This exalted the supposedly exclusive and specific nature of "Francism", which was necessarily Christian and exclusive. The other was the Jewish tendency, rooted in the past and in the international, Jewish community. Fleg was to adopt the guise of apologist for Jewish existence, even if that, locally, took on French garb and character. It is from this time onwards that he begins to express regrets that he had not devoted sufficient attention hitherto to the study of "his race, its history, and its actual position in the world."[6] There is no implication here that he wanted to break off relations with his friend, but only that he did recognise, as he formulated it in a letter to him, that "no intellectual accord is possible between us."[7]

Fleg did not immediately change the course of his writing in order to devote himself primarily to the expression of the Jewish cause. This was to occur some years later. And we can see from a casual glance at his chronological bibliography, that from a period somewhat predating the Great War and following the birth of his son, Maurice, (October 6 1908), he had effected a sea change by this later

---

5. Fleg indicates the closeness of his relationship to his mother in a letter that he wrote to her on May 23 1896. See the Fleg archive at the Alliance Israélite.
6. See his letter to Lucien Moreau (7 December 1898) as reproduced in Andre E. Elbaz (ed.) *Correspondence d'Edmond Fleg pendant l'affaire Dreyfus*. Libraire A.G.Nizet. Paris, 1976. All the translations here are my own (LIY).
7. Ibid. Letter of December 7 1898.

stage. The move was gradual, involved with momentous events. The war precipitated him not only into bloody conflict, but into a confrontation with his priorities and loyalties. From this point onwards, he was to be interested in the acquisition of French nationality (he had volunteered for army service as a Swiss citizen). The birth of his son by his wife, Madeleine Bernheim, (whom he married on December 9 1907), also focused his mind on the issue of historical continuity. This, for him, was expressed in the sense of Jewish life through the centuries. But it had been the Dreyfus Affair that had acted as a catalyst in this departure. And what happened to Fleg happened to many others too. It became clear to many hitherto emancipated and assimilated Jews, that, a hundred years after the revolution, the Jews were still not fully integrated into French life, and so not accepted naturally as a total part of the body politic. Universal implications also followed, as it was assumed that, in the field of human rights and political culture, France served as a model for the whole world.

What is quintessential to Fleg's approach is the involvement of his life with his literary expression from this point on. Whereas, as a literary aesthete, he had delighted in the creation of fine form, of objectification and the emotional distance from his creation, he now substituted an alternative touchstone; experiential truth with historical validification. *Why I am a Jew* is an existential memoir, which takes his own experience, sometimes painful and negative, as the starting point for the conduct of an investigation into himself and his manner of living. But he had to import into this expression all the layers of his own feeling life, if he were to be true to his conviction. And this feeling life included multiple attractions, feelings for France despite his anger, attachment to Lucien despite his friend's acknowledged anti-Semitism, in fact, a sense of dual attachment that was to become a fixture in his makeup, and which he was to acknowledge in his confessional statements to a theoretical future grandson.[8] Historically conditioned, he felt condemned to suffer this inevitable and continuing conflict.

---

8. In fact, no such grandson was to be born. His first son, Maurice, was to die in battle in World War 2 (June 29 1940), and his second son, Daniel, had committed suicide at the end of the previous year.

Fleg's Writing

Following the author's own method, the layers of consciousness as revealed in his literary expression have to be peeled off in order to create an effective encounter with the truth. But what is the truth? The truth exists both out there and within, but the latter is unreliable and changeable, subject to passing passions and fashions. Nevertheless, subjectivity is the only tool available, and in order to arrive at his most telling assessment of what should be a permanent, historical truth, he presents himself, i.e. his own subjectivity. And in *Pourquoi je suis juif,* he decides that if he wants to answer the explicit question of why he is a Jew, he has to begin by addressing the issue of why he was not a Jew previously, or, more precisely, why he ceased being such.

There is a generic issue of definition at stake here. The book looks like an autobiography, as it summarises his life hitherto (he was 53 years old at the time of its composition), and does detail his biography. On the other hand, it is an autobiographical account with a purpose, which is expressed in the title. So, every element extraneous to the declared objective is to be excluded. It is not a conventional autobiography, but a personal statement, an "apology" for his commitment to a declared position that emerges from personal circumstances, presented in the light of contemporary history, within a dialectical mode. First, there is the thesis, the statement of situation, then the challenge, which is followed by a counter challenge and resolution. This last stage takes the form of: I am a Jew because.... He concludes with a summary of faith existent, then lost, and finally regained more vitally.

The book, like others to follow, is written in the consciousness of future continuity. He is aware, not only of the two sons that he had, but of generations as yet unborn. So he addresses a future grandson, the guarantor of that continuity. Judaism is a religion based on history. It is an account of the generations and of a revelation carried forward by tradition. Without the family, in the broad sense of the word, encompassing tribal connections, bearing that tradition, the religion would not exist. The children of Israel are not only the witnesses to God; but, without this witness, God would have no meaningful existence, according to the Rabbinic message. And yet, he opens his account by saying, that, at the age of 20, he thought that he would have no further connection with Israel.[9] He writes in the same place: "I was persuaded that Israel was going to disappear, that one would no longer be speaking of Israel in twenty years' time."[10] This is the most total negation of what was to become the bedrock of his mental and spiritual being. But it serves as a suitable starting point for his testimony.

The author derives an important insight from his own retailed story. It is that the story does not just apply to himself, seemingly. It also approximates the story of the whole Jewish people. Israel's story too goes in fits and starts, gets moving at one point in history, and then seems to come an end further on, and is then reborn, although perhaps in another form and with many differences. So Fleg's own life becomes a paradigm for the story that he is trying to tell, and the two tales, the personal and the general, become intertwined. He says to the unborn grandchild that this might well happen for him too in the future. That is the overall lesson, one that he states as a primary thesis, before he actually recounts the events of his own life, a life that began in Geneva.

What had happened in Geneva, where he was born, was that, not only did he grow up of and into Jewish stock, but that he lived a life that was exclusively and separately Jewish. This he found restrictive and oppressive, and early contacts with other people and opinions were like a breath of fresh air for the curious adolescent. The hitherto self-sufficient world of the traditional Jew suffered a challenge just by the mere fact of contact. By comparison with the world outside, the Jewish tradition seemed to come a very poor second. For someone who was beginning to study Latin, and thus by implication the glories of alternative civilisations, the Hebrew that was offered seemed paltry and despicable. He was told, for example, that the language had no grammar (!). Everything related to his Jewish environment began to suffocate with its low level of achievement,

---

9. "Israel" is used here in the inclusive as well as the theological sense, referring to the Jewish people in its totality, past, present and future.
10. See Edmond Fleg, *Pourquoi je suis juif*. New edition. Les Belles Lettres. Paris, 1995. p.4.

particularly when seen in the light of the enticing new world on the outside. This constituted an early lesson in relativism; it is difficult to make a value judgement until you have something with which to compare. Things do not easily exist in a vacuum.

But the young Edmond, then aged 14, had the requisite talent to make a leap into another world. He could play the piano, so he became a regular guest of his neighbour's, something that would otherwise not necessarily have been the case. And, it was there that he became aware of what seemed to be another world altogether.

It was at this point that the apparent contrast between unthinking, routine practice became manifest. The practices with which he was so familiar; ritual observances, the Sabbath, the taboos, the forbidden foods etc. began to seem arbitrary and absurd. Strangely enough, he claims that what took him away from all that was the reading of the New Testament.[11] The reading of this work led him to despise the people for whom Jesus had evinced such contempt, with their contemporary counterparts in those who followed the path of legalistic Judaism. It was in the wake of this that he became a sceptic, and this sequence seemed to him to imitate the direction of modern thought, and, in Paris, became identified with a group of aesthetes.

He simultaneously noted that his own family observances (within the period that he spent at home) had become rather more lax, so confirming him in his own distancing from traditional practice. But, following the estrangement, the affinity with the personality of Jesus, and then the aestheticised scepticism, his equilibrium was then shattered by the Dreyfus Affair. This public event became a personal trial.[12] His mental life became revolutionised. The mark of the aesthete was both distance from public and communal concerns and supreme egoism. He claims to have discerned the innocence of Dreyfus immediately. But, further, the questions posed to the Captain became his own, i.e. questions addressed to him as well. But he saw these questions judaised and formulated as: "Jew, what is your place in the world?"[13] The rest of the book, and, in effect, of the principal

---

11. Ibid. p.19.
12. Ibid. pp.41, 42.
13. Ibid. p.43.

direction of his literary life, is an attempt to come to grips with this question, and to create a reply. He begins to regret his previous and current concerns, and to seek to replace them with an investigation of historical Judaism, together with its role in present day life. Almost simultaneously and consequently, public events provided some sort of response to the question, an antithesis to the thesis. This took the form of the incipient Zionist Movement, whose founding congress had taken place in 1897, and whose third congress he attended in 1899. It was following this that he declared that he was fated to bear forever a divided heart: 'a Jewish heart and a French heart.'[14] He would never recover the sense of simplicity that had been implied, firstly, in his ancestral home in Geneva, and, secondly, in his uncompromising rejection of that tradition as a sceptic in his early Parisian years. In the wake of the influences that we have observed here, he was to be drawn by Christianity, and later by French nationalism.[15] The more permanent reintegration into a more complex version of the initial Judaism was to remain modified and coloured by the later layers of loyalty, attraction and reason. But this he sees as his necessary condition, a condition which may well be carried forth into successive generations. He can not be sure, and it is for this reason that he poses the question to the future denizen of two generations beyond his own.

My Palestine

A further expression of this concern for future generations follows from his earlier declaration of faith (*Pourquoi je suis juif* is a credo of sorts, although it may not take that form throughout). A new sense of fate and association, not only with a Jewish historical line, but with a sense of renewed response and potential for the Jewish people, is expressed once more. The implied practical commitment had been to join and further the cause of the Zionist Movement. Fleg had joined early, and become an active enthusiast. The sense of

---

14. See Elbaz op.cit.
15. See his first play, *Le Message*, performed at the Nouveau Theatre, 1904.

obligation that flowed from that association was to the renewed Land of Israel, to the rebuilding of the country, which was, in the wake of World War 1, to come under the protection of Britain as a mandated territory, the furtherance of Jewish emigration there, the setting up of appropriate Jewish, national institutions, the interest in cultural revival, including that of the Hebrew language and literature, and the promotion of the Hebrew language as a vernacular. Fleg felt himself committed unambiguously to the Zionist programme, although, as we have seen, he still felt himself to be unambiguously French as well, and, therefore, a divided soul.

The book that followed some years later takes up this story. It is not only about Palestine (what the Jewish loyalist would refer to as the Land of Israel), but it is called "My Palestine".[16]

This indicates the now familiar intermingling of the external and the internal, the objectified fact and the personal, existential experiencing of that fact. The subject is not only the Land but "My Land". And the addressee is once again not the general reader of the Fleg opus, but, once more, the as yet unborn grandchild. This only reinforces both the centrality of the theme, seen as a continuity, linking past with present and future, but also the link between Fleg's experience of Jewish life, his historical knowledge and reconstruction of that life, historically, geographically and spiritually, and the shaping of the future. What Fleg was to view in Palestine, in 1931, was just as much about the future as a piece of immediate and present reportage.

Characteristically, the book opens with a recognition of ambiguity and ambivalence. "Palestine" flows dialectically from the whyness of being a Jew. But, it is also a place, with all the specificity of the word. It is located in the Middle East, not in Europe. It is underdeveloped in comparison with Europe, and, above all, it is necessarily and inevitably very different from France. So he opens his book on Palestine, paradoxically, with a declaration of love for "Paris on the Seine". But that Paris is dominated by the great cathedral of Notre Dame, which centres on the figure of Jesus, a Jesus ignored by his own people. This, he could have added, is

---

16. *Ma Palestine*. Paris, 1932. A Hebrew translation, by Aharon Amir, was published in Israel in 1957, am hasefer, which is the version referred to here.

complemented by the fact that the organisation emerging from that figure, in its turn, rejected, spurned and tormented the people from which the founder emerged. The Paris that Fleg loved, in other words, held a contradiction in its heart that also touched the heart of the author. Fleg seemed to become a man and a writer of contradictions, existential contradictions and opposites, which he could not or would not ignore, but rather attempted to pursue painfully to the ultimate. And so he goes to Palestine, in pursuit of himself, but knowing and declaring the attachment to his beloved home city (as it now was for him), and wondering whether there could ever be an additional home for such a visitor, so heavily imprinted with this existing attachment.

He also immediately spots a further paradox. As one who can not abide nationalists in Paris, is he to become that very thing in Jerusalem?[17] There is always the possibility that his line is going to be inconsistent, so that his ideology will encounter distortions, so that his very soul will be more divided than ever. This relates to the original internal dilemma over his identity; Frenchman or Jew, with all that is entailed by the interrogative. But, in the new Palestine, there are other virtues encountered. For the first time, he tells us, in Tel Aviv he feels free of the fear of anti-Semitism. Which is strange, as he also claims that he had never been conscious of that fear previously, in Paris. But that is the difference between conscious and unconscious. He now tends to believe that there had been this unconscious dread preying on his unconscious mind, and that he had been unaware of it. This is the sometimes unacknowledged, historical load, which he can shed here in this new Jewish country. And, in this presumably, is expressed the primary object and justification of the enormous enterprise now under way. Nevertheless, he is distressed by a sense of alienation. He does not feel totally integrated, less so, in fact, than others who had been welcomed as Jewish guest artists, such as Chagall and Patai. He does not, at this point, speculate on the possible reasons. But perhaps, a contributory factor might have been the fact that these other two were East Europeans, with a deep Judaic culture imbided from childhood, whereas he was a Westerner,

17. Ibid.pp. 76/77.

educated according to modern European norms, and according to the contemporary Western model.

For the political and cultural context, we should remember that Palestine was a territory that the British were holding as overseers in order to bring about "A Jewish National Home". This was not their exclusive task, as there were inevitably other responsibilities too, and, as we of course know from the record in retrospect, this primary purpose was to become increasingly compromised, bogged down, and even, to some extent, negated. But Fleg was nevertheless very excited by the prospect. This could be the appropriate counterfoil to the Dreyfusards, and even welcomed by the French nationalists who could accept the legitimate expression of nationalism on the part of the Jews. But the author could not help looking on both sides of the coin. All this effort, and just to create one more nation, only smaller? So, he is still divided. He is charmed by the expectation, entranced at the new vitality evinced by the ancient, tormented and degraded people of which he is a part. He is also curious at the religious implications implicit here, with a new type of faith being created. But, on the other hand, he is still basically French, in culture, language and habit. He is animated by the thought that this is the Land of Jesus and his ministry, Jesus, whom he regards as a great Rabbi and teacher in the Jewish tradition. But, on the other hand, perhaps the place of Jesus is now, more authentically, Rome, with the centuries of a different, accumulated cult. Palestine fills him with excitement for what it can offer, and the concrete reality of Biblical presence, which now presents itself in concrete guise. In summary, he assumes the character of the figure, semi-historical, semi-mythical, of the "wandering Jew". This label has been used pejoratively by the anti-Jews, who see that fate as a just punishment for the rejection of the Son of God. But, for Fleg, this is a figure of fascination, and a force that moves into the scientific era, and so into the twentieth century, with its revival of Jewish nationalism. The author returns to Paris in effect with his two obsessions enhanced, with that of the figure of the historical Jesus and with that of the wandering Jew. He has not resolved his inner contradiction, but brought it home in a mode reinforced.

Literary Typologies

Fleg set out on his career as a multi media author, poet, playwright and prose writer. As we have seen, he was to discover his metier in stages, under the influence of the Dreyfus Affair, then his marriage and the birth of his son, and then the Great War. It was these events that put him in mind of a larger time scale and the perspective of history. He illustrated conflicts, resolved and taken a stage further, in his work. Naturally, these were conflicts that reverberated in his own life, but they were projected on to his characters, and developed in the course of the created opus.

In his "drawing room play", *Le Trouble-Fête,*[18] he draws affluent, middle class characters, whose principal concern in life is to have a good time. Lise, the wife, and Julien, her husband-writer, each make the other the excuse for not having a child. Lise argues that: "we live in a century where one is less constricted". As for Julien: "he a coquet pampered by women, a dilettante...one who makes his life into an art, and has no taste for anything ugly." Lise feels little trust in the long term, thinks him brittle and changeable, and says that she is quite certain that if he were incarcerated alone with her, without outside distractions, he would come to hate her quite soon. That, even she admits, is the nature of the aesthete, one without deeper feelings, and without a longer term view. But, when she announces her pregnancy, he seems to change: "perhaps, this is something that we need, in order to become ourselves." In effect, though, he can not face the new routine imposed by life with a child, and, in the meantime, Lise is transformed and has become totally wrapped up in her maternal role. And then, the epilogue again shows the principal character cogitating the meaning of his existence, and considering his paternal status and love as determinant factors in his new makeup.

Truth is not something that exists as an autonomous factor, independent of its context and its container. Things are not external to the subject, somewhere out there, but shaped by our own subjectivity and circumstances. And the self is not necessarily

---

18. Librairie Théâtrale. Paris, 1913.

comprehended and understood by the ego. So, in order to know what we are, we have to become something else, in conformity to a life cycle. In his discovery of self, the author, Fleg, had to go through the processes of maturation. Firstly, there was the formative childhood experience, then the distancing, the learning, the perspective. Then came the blows of history, and the renewed consciousness of national and familial links. And the personal reinforcement developed with his own situation, that of marriage and procreation, situating him within a historical continuum. History became a paradigm of his life, and his life illustrated the broader tableau. His fictional characters too are existential types. Both Lise and Julien discover themselves through what transpires, through what happens to them, even though that had been unexpected and even unwanted.

Figures of the past too, in Fleg's dramas, emerge and become themselves, when projected by outside forces. Salomon Molco (1500-1532) was adopted by Fleg as a literary and ideological prototype for several reasons. He was born under the name of Diego Pires in Lisbon, as a descendant of Marranos, i.e. from a line of converts to Christianity from Judaism, into an environment where Jewish practice was forbidden. It was only following his encounter with the messianic figure of David Reuveni that Molco converted back to Judaism. He then went to Rome after it had been sacked by the Turks in 1527, and sought the protection of the Pope, Clement VII, after he had made prophecies which were later confirmed. He proclaimed himself Messiah, and was then condemned by the Inquisition for Judaising. He was first saved through papal intervention, but then, later, condemned to the stake by the Emperor, Charles V, in Mantua.

It seems clear that what appealed to Fleg in this story were the twin motifs of self-discovery and Messianic yearning. Fleg wrote the play, *Le Juif du Pape* [19], based on the meeting between Molco and the Pope. We have seen that the author was interested in the meeting of Judaism and Christianity, and that had foreshadowed his own personal encounter with the historical figure of Jesus. For Fleg, the

---

19. Written, January - March, 1924, and performed for the first time on October 28, 1925, at the Théâtre des Arts by the Compagnie Pitoeff. It was first published in 1925 and reprinted in 1958.

encounter between the two was authentic, not distorted by worldly power or threat. Clearly, the two faiths were not isometric; the Vatican was an enormous international force, whereas Judaism was physically nugatory, repressed, and at best, tolerated in temporary spurts. But, this could have been seen as a point in history where the two faiths might have come together, with the loyalists to the Church welcomed back into the Jewish fold, and the Jews accepting Jesus as one of their great representative Rabbis and as a prophetic figure.

Not all the best known features of Molco's life story are brought into Fleg's play. Technically, like many of Fleg's plays, it is composed in verse, mainly alternating between abab and aabb rhyme schemes. It is set in Rome, heralding the meeting between the two men, and the larger historical context is the appointment of the new Pope, the expectation of a renewed attack by the Turks, and thus the realisation on the part of the Pope that the Christian world has to unite in the face of adversity. Whilst, it may sound a little absurd to us, and even pretentious, Molco offers his own alliance to the Pope. This is made possible by the times in which they were living, i.e. in the expectation of the coming of the Messiah. Moses and Jesus can be united, when the Messiah comes. Molco also makes the claim that the ten lost tribes have been discovered, and so, with this, Jewry has been renewed, and is now a force to be reckoned with.

The basic difference between Judaism and Christianity, as Fleg sees it, is summed up by the two leading protagonists in the play. Molco says that he is awaiting the Messiah, and that he has not yet arrived; the Pope argues that the Messiah (i.e. Jesus) has already come, and that he will return. In a nutshell, the division seems to be one of timing, rather than of principle. After all, both faiths, and their chief representatives, accept the fact of Messiahship, implying divine rule, historical development and context, the principle of the good, and human agency. One could say further that both locate the source of revelation in Hebrew scripture, Biblical history and the Scriptural account as the source, the Holy Land as the prime scene of operations, the Jewish people as the messenger as well as the first object of the message. Jesus clearly was reared and taught in the Rabbinic tradition. And, for both, the origin is still to be located where it first emerged. So, the points of division would seem to be less significant than those of contact. Nevertheless, the two protagonists, who are also here advocates of unity, meet ultimate hostility from within their own camps. The Jews see Molco as an apostate, seeking common ground with the Christians. Is he not in fact acting as a back door Christian through this illicit activity? Likewise, the Christians are suspicious of Molco, and are not happy with the Pope's sympathy, a fact that is born out by later developments, as we know them. The play in fact ends, not at the point of rupture, nor with Molco's proclamation of his Messiahship. It concludes rather with the agreed declaration of common purpose, allowing for the differences, and hoping for a happier future, where: "Perhaps one day, over the war in the world,/ Peace will take on the name of a Roman pontiff;/ Perhaps one day, in order to raise the world once more,/ Rome and Jerusalem will join hands;"[20] The Pope's own compromise is to suggest unity whilst allowing for separateness. As he says: "Let the two of us stay united, yet both alone,/ In order to travel together, we must split up!"[21] For his part, Molco asserts in his final speech: "Whatever be the way, the light is at the end./ Let us walk then towards the day, where the shade stutters forth,/ A future day, in which the present is remembered:/...For blackest night is a coming dawn!"[22]

The contemporary allusions for a work written by Fleg in 1913 are manifold. War is imminent, and can only be countered with some sort of spectacular (Messianic) expectation. The themes of Christianity being imbibed and accepted by Judaism are incorporated, as well as the millennarian vision. But this is all within the context of the post-Enlightenment world. Not included in the play are Molco's own (alleged) claims to being the Messiah nor his own stated belief in the miracle of his own conversion back to Judaism and the sudden acquisition of Rabbinic and Hebraic knowledge.[23] Excluded is the miraculous element, in favour of the plausible and the contemporaneously relevant, as well as the concern for reconciliation between the faiths and the search for peace.

---

20. Ibid. p.155.
21. Ibid.
22. Ibid. p.156.
23. See the introduction to Molco's *sefer hamfoar* (1529, reprinted in 1993, Jerusalem).

Jesus, the Wandering Jew and the Teaching

The investigation into the life and the teachings of Jesus continued for Fleg throughout his life. But the purpose of the research was to reintegrate Jesus and the Church that emanated from him once more back into Jewish history. After his initial attempt to locate him in his context during the year 1931, he returns to offer a more concentrated report on this single subject, on Jesus as related by the wandering Jew.[24] This would locate Jesus within the Holy Land, in Jerusalem, at the height of the period of the Second Temple, following the emergence of Judaism as a crystallised religion, constructed around a nation living, albeit under a foreign power, in its own country. Fleg, to a greater and greater extent, was not just interested in creating a fiction of the historical Jesus, but also in reconstructing the story as precisely as possible, according to all the available sources, Jewish, Christian and Roman. But the construction of the narrative is built on a dialogue between the narrator, who wants to discover for himself what happened, and his guide in this strange territory, who turns out to be "the wandering Jew". The "book" (it is difficult to characterise this work generically, composed as it is in the form of a journal, fictionalised, but with a scholarly apparatus) has a comprehensive concordance appended, with precise references to the available sources. It is also written from two chronological perspectives, from that of the time of composition in 1932, and from that of its presumed setting, at the time of Jesus himself. This offers the twin advantages of a sharpened sense of realism on the one hand, and a distant, objectified and more informed perspective, on the other. The figure of the Wandering Jew too creates a link between the centuries, as this figure belongs both to past and to present, to history and mythology. It is a figure that is quintessentially Jewish, diasporic with its origins in Palestine, one that belongs to the consciousness of the whole people and also peculiarly, to the author himself.

---

24. *Jesus raconté par le juif errant.* Editions Albin Michel. Paris, 1953. First published in Paris, 1933.

This wandering Jew figure is full of indignation. What he wants and expects is immediate redemption, fulfilment of the messianic prophecy. Not that it should be postponed until some time in the vague future, but for now, in our own time. What is the Christian origin of the notion of the wandering Jew? He (i.e. the figure who is telling the story to the narrator) was present at the crucifixion, and, after Jesus had fallen, whilst bearing the cross, for the third time, was asked to bear his cross. Whereupon Jesus said: "Since you refuse to bear my cross, until I return ...you will wander!"[25] This, as we see in regard to other aspects of the story, is based on a source, here the Gospel of John 21:22., and it is at this point that the narrator realises that his interlocutor is taking himself for the Wandering Jew.[26] But, in punishment for his initial refusal, he now has to bear the cross whenever he passes by this way. And this suffering creature tells his astonished auditor that what is happening is a reality, and that the Wandering Jew is not just a legend, repeated as a fiction for later generations. In fact, one of the principal points that he makes is the distinction between that time and this (i.e. between the first and the twentieth centuries). Then, the expectation of the "coming" was not just a phrase, but a perceived reality, filling all one's mental space. In modern times, everyone knows that the Messiah is not going to come. Waiting for the Messiah at that time was rather like the hope for peace on the part of those fighting in the trenches during the Great War. It took over everything else. He then goes on to tell the story.

But Fleg was a synthesiser. Even in recounting the ancient story of Jesus, he sought an additional contemporary perspective, as well as to integrate it into a full Jewish perspective, linking up the chronology, the mythology, and the linking leitmotif of the Wandering Jew, holding the generations together. But Jewish history altogether, from his perspective, was taking on a wholeness. From Biblical revelation and the original Jewish story, through loss, exile

---

25. Ibid. p.17.
26. The so-called source is of course just a prooftext for a legend that originated many centuries later (the first recorded reference to the developed form of this story, with the anti-Jewish archetype is 13th. century Bologna). The Jew who refused to bear the cross for Jesus is condemned to live and wander until the second coming of Jesus.

and Diaspora, with the varying forms of Jewish expression throughout the world, and, now, at the very present moment of his old age, there was taking place a precarious but apparently semi-miraculous renaissance of the Jews in their ancient land, now reinforced by the political form, publicly and internationalised recognised, of a new State. At this moment, Fleg both welcomed the birth of this State, and also sought a new synthesis. In a pamphlet, expressing this desire, "The Problem for Today",[27] he returns to a theme prefigured in the Jesus book above. The Wandering Jew expresses impatience at the vagueness of the messianic expectation, and demands immediate fulfilment. Now, some decade and a half later, Fleg has personally discerned the concrete signs of that messianic realisation. And with this, there is to be a further reassessment of Jewish history. Emancipation in republican France was bought at the price of the surrender of Jewish nationality. But now, argues Fleg, this anomaly is to be removed. Those wanting Jewish nationality can opt for it, whilst those in favour of French nationality will have nothing to do, from the point of view of self-identification, with that national revival in Palestine.

But synthesis is to be laid on synthesis. The Jewish nation has always been multi-layered, of many times and places, and so it is bound to remain. The Jewish nation, in total, should combine the particularism of the State with the universalism of its historical and geographical experience. It would be idolatry to worship the State as such, since, as the Bible itself attests, the Land, like all lands, belongs to God. There is always a higher, universal authority. Jewish history informs us that, although the specific territory was the focus, it was neither the sole scene of operations, nor the source of revelation for its founding fathers. Abraham came from outside, Moses was never there. The Babylonian Talmud has greater range and attraction than the Jerusalem Talmud. The founding document of Zionism, *The Jewish State*, was composed in Vienna, as was a great deal of its major literature, even that written in Hebrew. So Judaism still belongs everywhere and will continue to do so, even though an immediate and urgent political issue seems to have been resolved.

---

27. Edmond Fleg. *Le problème d'aujourd'hui*. Fondation sefer. Paris, 1948.

One of the principal ambitions that Fleg was constantly realising was that of anthologising. The anthology was another form of synthesis, combining past with present, all cultures and languages, and being constantly updated. There is no more majestic achievement than the *Jewish Anthology*[28] , which attempted to present something of Jewish creativity and spirit throughout the generations, up to the moment of composition.. It was in this spirit no doubt that he was honoured by a group in his city of origin, Geneva, in 1950, to render a performance of his play, *Le juif du pape*, and a reading of his poems, in honour of the person whom they regarded as their spiritual father.[29] Fifty eight years after his departure from Geneva, he was recalled and memorialised, whilst he was still struggling in an attempt to find a home somewhere or other. Maybe Geneva, perhaps Paris, or a step towards Jerusalem? Or all of these places together, and beyond?

---

28. Edmond Fleg (ed.) *Anthologie juive: des origines à nos jours*. Flammarion. Paris, 1951. This first appeared in 1923, and was supplemented and reedited several times.
29. See letter to Fleg from Borah Fradkoff. From Edmond Fleg Archive at the Alliance Israélite, Paris.

V

IS AHARON APPELFELD A HOLOCAUST WRITER?

Recent Writing

Until the Dawn's Light[1] follows in the tradition of *Katerina,*[2] in its epic scope, its tight, action packed, sequential narrative, its pace and its violence.[3] Appelfeld's stories have taken two forms; one slow moving, brooding, with the omniscient narrator passing judgment, and the reader then predicting the inevitable outcome, with the principal protagonists adopting fixed postures. The other moves the narrative on quickly, even impatiently. *Until the Dawn's Light* is of the second type. But here the texture is thicker than the author's earlier fictions of this type, more filled out. It is set in the first decades of the century, in a remote region of Austria. The narrative is filtered principally through the eyes of the young heroine, who was, when young, a brilliant Jewess, outstanding academically in her class of mainly jealous Christians. The atmosphere is one where Christianisation is rampant, and indeed seen as the key to success and social acceptability. She too is caught up in the whirl of the times, evincing contempt for an outworn faith, and putting a misplaced reliance on a

---

[1] Aharon Appelfeld, *Ad sheyaaleh hashahar.* (Until the Dawn's Light). Keter. Jerusalem, 1995.

[2] Aharon Appelfeld, *Katerina.* (Katerina). Keter. Jerusalem, 1990.

[3] Everything here is based on the Hebrew editions of the author's work. Any quotations refer, in brackets following, to the Hebrew source in my own translation.

plodding classmate who cannot cope with Latin or Mathematics. She, out of social conscience and empathy, seeks to help this inarticulate brute, and then accepts his offer of marriage.

This is the source of her tragedy. She converts, and becomes his house slave, violently exploited and beaten. She has a child, Otto, who becomes the focus of her whole life, and for whom she is writing her memoirs. At first, she accepts her lot passively, partly out of the recognition that her fall stemmed from her own mistaken notions and gullibility, and partly out of terror. She even takes an outside, menial job, which entails leaving her home throughout the week, virtually abandoning her beloved child, and surrendering her husband to a local wench, who fills in, looking after the child and the house, that is to say, stripping her of her last remaining hold on life. All builds up to the violent climax within a violent setting.

The story is told on two time scales. One is the present, ongoing time, with the heroine in desperate straits, fleeing the Law after murdering her husband, taking her child with her, but then leaving him to the care of a benign educational institution. The other scale is of the material of the journal, which she wants to entrust to her son. This is made up of a description of how she arrived at this condition, the sympathy for the boorish, the entrapment, the denial of her Jewish roots, the hostility of the alien environment, and, finally, the despair leading to murder and flight. She had not been able to care for her helpless father, and she is determined now to do her best for her little boy. She has reached the stage where she hankers for her roots, in the place of her birth, that region where the Baal Shem flourished, (as she learns from Buber's *Tales*), the Carpathians. And it is in the course of her flight, which is accompanied by increasingly violent behaviour, that she is finally caught by the police. But, at this point, she is virtually indifferent to her present condition, and only longs for her father and the cafe where they used to sit.

In a recent study, Yigal Schwartz has categorized Appelfeld's work under three headings.[4] These are: the attempt to recapture and restore the author's childhood; the "broad expanse of a literary king-

---

[44] Yigal Schwartz, *Kinat hayahid venetsah hashevet.* (Individual Lament and Tribal Eternity). Keter. Jerusalem, 1996.

dom"; the religious stance of the narrator, the relationship between the Jewish world (that of the tribe and its faith) and the encroaching gentile world. *Until the Dawn's Light* belongs to the third category. Its main theme, obsessively recurrent, is the immutable and persistent character of an ancient kernel of Jewishness, which is always at the back of the mind of the chief protagonist, however difficult its satisfactory formulation. This sense is indeed the common theme of all Appelfeld's fiction, whatever the place or time setting, and however the narrative is filtered.

Appelfeld's Subject

Whatever the apparent setting of the author's fiction, whatever the decade, there persists a consistent view of the subject. The settings do indeed vary, from the central Europe of the first decade of the century, to the Austria of the 30s, from the period immediately preceding the war and the Holocaust, to the transit following the war for the survivors. Pre-Israeli Palestine and Israel are also the scenes for the setting of some of the stories. But there is a remarkable indifference to external realia, to the current scene, to the concerns of other sections of the population. In the post-war setting, the protagonists remain frozen in the attitudes, psychic and mental, that had been acquired earlier. The Holocaust has frozen them into fixed positions. But we also find that the Holocaust has not, so it seems, wrought a fundamental transformation of postures, only confirmed them. The typical Appelfeld protagonist learns from his experience in the world that his encounter can only bring about rediscovery of the Jewish element, whatever that may be and however it may be seen. Thus, ironically, although the Holocaust has cast its shadow both forward, where the survivors are now transfixed, and backwards, to those who operate within the framework of an impending doom, one known at least to the reader, it does not change the situation, but only confirms it. Appelfeld has in fact, until recently in his novel, *The Ice Mine*,[5] which represents a departure in its explicitness and direct

---

[55] Aharon Appelfeld, *Mikhreh hakerah.* Keter. Jerusalem, 1997.

treatment of the camp experience, never treats directly of the period between 1939 and 1945. He rather assumes it as an entity known. The representation of the documentary truth, the factual account of the horror, can, on the whole, be left to others, to historians, to chroniclers, to writers of different types. Appelfeld perceives his function differently. It seems to be to get under the skin of the historical personality of the Jew in the modern world, to discover the psychic reality of the "tribe". It may be ironic that the writer who is known as the Holocaust writer par excellence should, in fact, never have touched it directly, but rather skirted round delicately, leaving the horrific crassness to others. What an author of this special character might be able to achieve rather is a penetration into this permanent reality, living in the shadow of a world, where the Holocaust is only the most horrific and ultimate manifestation, but not one unique, unprecedented, or indeed perhaps, unrepeatable.

Variations in technique

Time is a significant operative in Appelfeld's stories. Some of the stories cover a very brief span, focusing on figures found in a given situation and frozen in them. Others cover a lifetime. *Katerina,* for example, is narrated by the central figure, and conveys the essence of her very long and eventful life. *Until the Dawn's Light* is proclaimed by the dust cover to be of that mould, rich in incident and external plot development. It is also a violent story, as we have seen. But there is a message in the tale, and the sting is in the violence. There is the violence perpetrated on the brutal husband, who is himself violent, and there is the violence done to the heroine brought on by her own denial; the lack of recognition of her own essence. As a result of the violence done to her, she herself becomes violent. But the initial action was her own, and it lay in a sort of self-deception. And this misunderstanding too came about as a result of circum- stances, to a large extent historically conditioned. Blanca is a Jewess, living on the borders of non Jewish society, seeing in her Jewish element merely negative connotations. From the standpoint of her parents' negative assessment of the Jewish part of her being and from her own assessment of the rights of man and the current situation, it would mean little to her, apparently, to sacrifice that small Jewish part, which, for her, was just an irritation. In this sense, the story line represents a further stage in the line of tradition of Enlightenment literature, and particularly of what is known as Vitalism, influenced, directly or indirectly, by Nietzsche. In Adolph Blanca discerns the lad for whom she displays sympathy and whom she is later to marry. She sees in him power and vitality. He is strong and untroubled by intellectual doubts and physical weakness. Just as the pathetic Jew emerging from the Pale was attracted to the natural rootedness of the gentile native, to his unencumbered physicality and free sexual expression, so is Blanca drawn to the apparently untroubled Adolph. These traits are apparent in his lack of academic prowess, which becomes, for Blanca a virtue rather than a failing, and her liberal sympathies allow her to view him as at least an equal. That this "vitality" is actually anti-Semitism, and that this was always present as an essential element of his makeup and culture would only become fully apparent in their life together. By denying her historical place, she is also denying herself. The tale thus unfolds as a necessary retribution, determined and justified by her wilful blindness. She goes to her Fate, at the engimatic and problematic conclusion of the novel, willingly. There is to be inherent justice in what awaits her. She has to suffer shame, the shame of a daughter not taking in her 53 year old father, the shame of a Jewess hating her Jewishness, the shame of a person not defending herself until she takes the drastic and ultimate step of killing her husband. No moderate way out was offered as a possibility. The shame of her non-recognition led to the shame of her conversion, to the shame of her betrayal and to the crime of murder. In the meantime, she takes revenge by burning down churches, whilst writing her memoirs (this book) for her child, whom she has protected above all else. The novel is a tale of return. Here, the Carpathian mountain region represents the actuality of her origins, and it is to that Land of the Baal Shem, founder of the Hasidic sect, an authentic tendency of Jewish revivalism, that she would return. But, before that can be achieved, she must pay the price both for her own shame and for the crime committed by society. As in Dostoevsky's *Crime and Punishment*, the criminal gives himself up. Self-surrender is more effective than discovery, because it involves self-knowledge and a willingness to put what has been learned into effect. The heroine offers a message in this version of the *Bildungsroman*, and there the story ends.

This novel obviously, in view of the narrative point of view, contains no reference to the Holocaust, and any implications for that event, or knowledge derived from it, would necessarily be indirect. It is set in the first decades of the century, before World War 1. Historically, we know that the Jewish communities of Europe still flourished, although, to some extent, their spiritual life was residual. Enlightenment had drawn the Jewish and Gentile worlds together, and there seemed little intelligent option for the smaller element than to be absorbed into the larger. But, if our claim is true, and the Holocaust is not the defining event in Jewish history, but rather the ultimate metonymy of loss, this account can be seen as an illustration of the depradation brought about by the modern situation. Our subject then is less clearly demarcated than might be thought. Denial can lead to hostility and to the violence of mutual destruction.

Post-Holocaust Fiction

One of the effects of the Holocaust on literature has been that it has brought about a situation which transcends the possibility of any sort of adequate representation. Any mimetic effort true to its subject would cease to be aesthetic production, literary material, and become gruesome chronicle. The literature that takes in the Holocaust, and any serious contemporary literature must take it in, in the sense that it remains at the base of its assumptions, has to go beyond representation of the facts, whilst of course still acknowledging their veracity. The Holocaust in Appelfeld, and as conveyed by the author himself in his own person, is the Holocaust of the child, without concrete memory. And, as there is no concrete memory, the traces cannot be erased.[6] Much of Appelfeld's fiction, as we have seen, is

---

[6] Aharon Appelfeld, *Masot beguf rishon*. (Essays in the First Person). The Zionist Library. Jerusalem, 1979, pp. 24, 25.

set in the post-war world, in the world of survivors, where these are the chief figures and the exclusive focus.

Does this make Appelfeld a Holocaust writer? Certainly, this is how he is regarded, although many take issue with this blanket categorisation, and hedge it with qualifications, even when partially accepted.[7] In the Foreword to the collection of essays entitled, appropriately, "Essays in the First Person", the author does specifically denote his theme as being "the relationship to the Holocaust". Indeed, this is one of the few occasions where this stance is explicitly invoked. But then, the genre is different, and so demands and creates patterns of its own. The title of the essay collection conveys this essential distinction. "The first person" is what it declares. This is no longer a fiction, where a world separate from the author is created, but the revelation of immediate and personal experience in relation to the Holocaust. The testimony is of the individual, the only one valid. Gershon Shaked has argued that the world of the author is indeed populated by figures who have emerged directly from the cauldron, not filtered by imagination nor by empathy, as is the case with other Israeli writers who have entered this territory.[8] But fiction is what it makes claims to be, an imaginative penetration into the world of the other. This is surely why fiction of any kind, but specifically that relating to the Holocaust is placed in disparate settings and in various periods. Even when the author deploys the first person narrator, it must clearly be grasped as a fictional device; that much can be seen by the crude device of checking such fictions against the author's own biographical data, and coming up with clear discrepancies. Autobiographical essays are in a different category from fictional narrative, and the reader response generated therefore varies in accordance with the nature of the expectations raised.

---

[7] See, for example, Alan Yuter, *The Holocaust in Hebrew Literature: From Genocide to Rebirth*. Associated Faculty Press. Port Washington. New York, 1983, where he argues that the author examines "...the residual effect of the Holocaust on its survivors", p.61, i.e. that he does not deal with the experience overtly, but rather with its later effect.

[8] Gershon Shaked, *Gal hadash basiporet haivrit*. (New Wave in Hebrew Fiction). Sifriyat poalim. Tel Aviv, 1970, p.79.

But again, in spite of the necessary caution that we must exercise in making a distinction between autobiography and fiction, even the fictionalised work remains close to a tapestry, a portrait of tribal Jewry, of which the author is part. He is witness to a scene, the portrait of a residual and terrorised people attempting to come to terms with the shock and trauma before moving on to wherever. The immediate post-war phase is a vital element in this overall panorama. The individuals and the collective bear the effects of what has passed, but they must also consider what is to come, and make preparation. This can be called the Italian phase, as it was in Southern, coastal Italy that a small group assembled, an assortment of survivors, supported by the "Joint", and described in important stories, such as "1946".[9] In this camp, near Naples, a cross section of this battered population awaits its fate. The story is saved from excessive metaphorisation by the narrative thrust. There is still a tendency to compare everything to something else, to characterise the "mournful melody" as being "full of evening", to picture the "striped coats" as "startled waves", but there is an urgent story to tell. We want to know about these people, how they have been affected, how they plan to shape their future, and where they are going to go.

But are they separate individuals, or do they constitute an indistinguishable mass? We read that: 'The warm darkness wiped all individuality from their countenances'. Of course, within the group people have names. There are adults, old and young, children, entertainers, the sick, the adventurers. And there are also the outsiders. An attractive woman is brought in, Stella, a local. Lump, through his infatuation, becomes young again. In the meantime, she is fascinated by the fate of the Jews.

We are immediately struck, in terms of narrative technique, by the fact that we are not taken up specifically with any particular individual's fate or story. As in *Badenheim,* the first story in the volume that contains two stories, we are presented with a section of a population, here, the tribe, and move from one to the other, as though dealing with a representative sample. The year, 1946, becomes a

---

[9] Published together with "Badenheim, ir nofesh" in *Shanim veshaot.* (Years and Hours). Hakibbutz hameuhad. Tel Aviv, 1975.

metaphor, and stands, together with the location, Italy, for the beginnings of the recovery (for the residue only, obviously). Italy in 1946 represents a kind of half-way point between the terror of repression and obliteration on the one hand, and the possibility of recovery, on the other. The people still bear the marks of the terror. Like animals, they still carry the traces of being hunted, and have not yet made their way back into human specificity. Appelfeld often characterises the unit as a "tribe". They stick together. Stella, the outsider, attempts to get hold of the nature of the collective, not of each individual. Lump, in his responses to her (she, after all, is his girlfriend) stresses the unique talents of each separate person. They had education, which means background and a private history. We are at a transitional stage between the undifferentiated animal horde and the normality of separate humans coming together voluntarily, but also going their own ways at will. Lump also sees himself as an animal in relation to Stella, and asks her why she ties him up when he wants to leave the camp. His freedom is expressed precisely in not knowing when he will return; that is the human element in his being, not to be bound like a dog. But what a motley crew is here in this random sample of few survivors; smugglers, illegal traders, and also, by the way, a Rabbi, held up as a model, and worshipped as a symbol. There is, however, an even deeper source of malaise. Any sign of life that is to be found in Lump now comes to him exclusively from the outside: 'Sometimes he felt that his existence was light as a feather. True life was embodied in Stella. As long as Stella stays with him he will live.

At night Stella would withdraw to the side, kneel down and pray. Lump knew suddenly, that everything in him had died. Maybe he was just a metamorphosis, a shadow attached for a moment to a live body' (116). A central feature of the survivor, picked up time and again in the literature, is the sense of death in apparent life.[10] The

---

[10] See for example the novel by Isaac Bashevis Singer, *Enemies: A Love Story* (originally published in the Yiddish journal, *Forverts*, New York, 1966), where not only the central figure, Herman Broder, feels that he is still inhabiting the hayloft which served as his home in Poland for three years during the war, but the other major figures, the lustful Masha and her mother Shifra-Puah only manage to hold on to a residual life through their mutual dependence. Herman's original wife, Tamara,

Italian camp acts as a mid-way staging post on the way back to some sort of re-entry into a new phase. There is little sense of contemporary reality within the group. Even when the place name, Palestine, begins to be heard within the camp, those who hear it do not relate to it as an actual place in the world, but only as a sound composed of syllables. The thought too that they might conduct a trial of two men who had probably betrayed them to the police (for smuggling) is thought to be virtually inconceivable. So rather than get down to the projected "trial", they just hold them, tied up. The question to be raised is: what is the Law, and what constitutes justice? Rather than confront the difficulty, they become virtually paralysed.

So, to what extent are Appelfeld's narratives populated by survivors specifically marked by the Holocaust? It is said of two of the young women that they are becoming more and more beautiful: ' "The war has not changed them in the least. They have the memory of ants." ' (This speech is unattributed, so presumably belongs, like so many of the utterances made in the stories, to the general collective.) And the reply comes back, from another unattributed source: ' "So what do you want them to do? Cry?" ' (129). An emergent view is that the events of the war are best forgotten, even at this early stage, as the memory of them can achieve nothing positive. Another response is to prepare in the direction of collective strength, for possible self defence and even nationhood. This is under the direction of the charismatic Franck, an outsider from what had been the Austrian army, held in suspicion as well as in awe by the Jews. He can restore some measure of self respect. If only that had existed a little earlier, they perhaps would not have been led like sheep to the slaughter! But it is too late now. In any case, it all belongs to the past, just as Judaism itself seems to belong to the past. Not unnaturally, they sometimes speak of the Jewish episode in History as though it is all over now. So, even if the Holocaust is not represented or even invoked directly, it remains a constant presence by implication.

We must return to the question of what the term "Holocaust writer" means. It can carry with it the connotations of direct descrip-

---

who he had thought dead, actually survived, but she is metaphorically and physically possessed by the bullet that had lodged in her.

tion of the physical act of destruction and extermination. That clearly does not happen here, as, even when the direct experience is related, that experience is of a "labout camp" rather than an extermination camp. On the other hand, it can also be interpreted as transmitting the effect of the event, its implications for what has gone before it, and what is to come in its wake. The fact of the Holocaust can modify our understanding of the Jewish situation preceding it, as well as shaping the fate of the remnants beyond. Much of Appelfeld's writing in this respect is indirect. It involves the reader who must know more than what is crassly set down on the page. But does not all writing carry certain shared assumptions and knowledge with the reader? In this instance, the reader is presumed to know what has happened. The Hebrew reader, certainly, bears it on his skin. "1946" transmits the implied heritage of the six previous years, and takes us beyond, into the collective psyche, where not all is overtly stated. But it still must be understood as Holocaust writing in this enlarged sense of the term. The two opposed views put forward by the protagonists in the story are: first, that the past should be remembered, recovered and revived; and second, that it is just as well to forget it all, with its misery, humiliation and suffering. Meanwhile, the remnants are few, and such as are left may well soon be dispersed, or disappear like water in the sand. Again, one possible reaction to this, as expressed here, is that this would be a positive upshot, as "'everyone bears within him the sting of poison'"(136). And the reaction expressed to the articulation of that tendency, is that there is no necessity to take steps to achieve that, as the disappearance will take place willy nilly. We do not have to bring it about. But this is but one tendency of various such; the respect due to the Rabbi, the pleasant, if rather vague connotations of Palestine, the awareness of the Day of Atonement, the new self respect that is now being acquired under the direction of Franck. But this is all in a state of flux, and may shift once more, as the foundations of such attitudes are so shaky. It is a decadent and almost extinct society, that can only be redeemed, and that in very small part, by the allure of a way out. The whole situation is interim. The respite is not decisive, but offers a pause following catastrophe, but before the unknown future. We have here the partial story of a group. As with *Badenheim*, there is no hero, no central figure, but the remnants of a society, the residue of the tribe. The story ends when the camp is dissolved, and they are picked up by boat to go on to the new destination. But, by the time they leave, they are severely depleted and reduced in every sense. Some had gone to other places in Europe, some to Australia, and others had mysteriously disappeared. It is a ragged medley, but one that suffers in its separate parts, dissolving into a mixture of despair and Messianic hope. By this time, there are only thirty two people left, including children and the sick, and they have nothing, no possessions of any kind. There is no resolution at the story's conclusion, although there is a demarcation of the end of a process.

Witness to Disaster

In order to grant a perspective to the events that dominate Appelfeld's opus, *Katerina* is narrated, unusually, by a gentile woman, who tells her story at the age of eighty. The perspective on the total narrative is gained by the fact that, within a relatively brief fictional space (132 pages of Hebrew text), a time span of several generations is covered, as well as a large geographical area. The story also takes us from the inter-war period, when stetl life still existed, although under threat, as far as the present moment, which means, through the most violent and destructive episodes of Jewish history. And all this is viewed both from within and without; from the standpoint of a participant and one who was involved, but also who was not actually Jewish. The author has adopted in this novel an unusually heavy disguise, an invention and imagined situation that adds to the power of the fiction. But we are back in the Land of the Cattails (Land of the Reeds), a characteristically Appelfeld locus, a very Jewish, primal and tribal scene. She, Katerina, has come to play out her last, and recall times past, for herself, and incidentally, for the reader too. Her story is full of incident and violence. So this is a family saga on an epic scale, compressed, where the narrator comes full circle, returning to the source of her life. The author returns to the cruelty and viciousness displayed towards women in his later novel, *Until the Dawn's Light*. But whereas that is a story about a highly educated Jewess, whose conscience leads her to assimilation-ist tendencies, here we have the gentile narrator actually attempting to get under the skin of her Jewish associates. The similarity between the two works lies in their scale, pace and variety; strong narrative features not always evinced in the author's work. There is a strong sense of locale, of association with the ethnic environment, and, especially in old age, with their religious roots. Here the tribe becomes manifest in individual sentiment, obliterating accumulated baggage and increments. The dead indeed exercise maximum control. The generations past necessarily tighten their hold over the present.

Initially, she left home in order to escape the primitive domination of her father and, especially, of her new stepmother. What really preserves Katerina is her belief in manifest destiny and in ultimate retribution. Everything that is done on earth will find its inevitable consequence. So, even if evil is done, it will be seen by God, who will exact recompense. When she left her home, she set out on what was known as "the Jewish path", a side road, and this seemed to confirm her fate as interlocked with that of the Jews, despite the general hostility evinced towards them on the part of her own people. They were associated with devils and feared as cheats. For example, it was not regarded as wrong to steal from them; her mother would tell her that you could steal from a thief with impunity. The Jews were another species, something derived from the fact that they had murdered Jesus. Her own life was to be one of degradation in the primitive rural heartland of the Ukrainian regions, starting out amongst the down and outs and beggars at the Strasov railway station, learning to steal and subsist as far as possible, like her associates there.

But Katerina is extricated from this life by a Jewish woman who takes her into her employ. It is from this point on that the absolute division between Jew and Christian begins to break down for her, and that she can begin to cross this terrifying divide. She moves into that other territory, and so can offer something of a dual perspective that marks out this narrative. She observes that on the part of the Jews too, the sense of otherness is perceptible and total. It is as though there are two quite distinct human species that eye each other with suspicion and loathing. She bears a child by a man whom later she can scarcely remember, suffers in childbirth, and struggles to nurse the baby. So her life now enters a new phase, and she succumbs more and more to the Jewish influence. She says that she became associated with them, without paying due attention to the fact (26). Although we still have a narrative transmitted from both sides of the fence, the gravity of sympathy shifts, and the narrator is now further entrenched in the Jewish camp, with all the guilt necessarily flowing from that self-identification with the Christ killers. A duality was to enter her soul, and divide her permanently. She no longer belongs unambiguously to one category or the other, and she is thus no longer capable of enjoying the simple pleasures that she once had experienced so vividly. She becomes even more attached to the family when, first the father, Benjamin, with whom she had fallen in love, and then, Rosa, the mother, were murdered by hooligans and mobsters. She devotes herself to the two children, who are later forcibly removed by Ruthenian agents of the relatives of the late mother. Now she has lost almost everything. She has abandoned her own baby, her protectors have been murdered, her charges have been snatched away, and she is alienated from her own origins.

But now she is redeemed for a second time by another Jewess, this time by one non-observant, one of the "modern" variety. But her stay there is brief, and again she returns to the inn, her first port of call, where she made her initial contact with the outside world. However, she is by this time so "infected" by her Jewish influence that she can no longer be absorbed into that earthy and primitive community. She must travel on, and so she continues to Czernowitz, whence her most recent employers had made tracks. But their ways part again, and again Katerina is left alone. It is a new Katerina and also a new environment. As one familiar and sympathetic, and specifically as a Yiddish speaker, she wants to and can mix freely with the downatheel Jews of this city, capital of the province of Bukovina. We are in the underbelly of urban life, amongst drunkards and beggars, amongst whom are many Jews, including her new comrade, Sammy. They drink together, live together, and soon she finds herself, much to Sammy's regret, pregnant. Her whole being is now bound up with her lovely little boy, whom she has circumcised and calls Benjamin, after her true love. Here, and in these circumstances, circumcision is likely to be a form of execution. But she insists, in spite of all the difficulties and refusals (after all, he is not Jewish), and so takes the critical step in initiating the child into this excruciating covenant. And the reason? Because her heart told her to, she says. In her new situation, she leaves the city, and once more sets out for the villages, to live a Jewish life, isolated, except with her child. There is murder all around, and she would like to insulate him, to create a cocoon of tranquillity. Yiddish will be his language.

But then the ultimate disaster occurs. Karel, an old acquaintance from her village, after plaguing her to abandon the child and go off with him, snatches Benjamin and crushes his head. In her anguish, she cuts Karel's throat with a household knife, not letting go until she is sure that he is dead. Thus, as she says, she ends the first half of her life. We cannot say that there has been no build up to the stark horror of the scene, but this, in its unfiltered brutality surpasses anything that has gone before. She says of herself that it is she who has now been murdered, with only the stump remaining (90). The prison regime to which she is submitted makes no impact on her. In prison, she is in an even better position to observe from afar and more objectively what is happening in normal, civil life. Rumours and stories abound about what is happening to the Jews. Their clothes and other property arrive at the prison to the unbridled joy of the recipients, spoils of the pogroms. The plunder and murder of the Jews did not await the Holocaust; it seems to have been continuing apace constantly, gaining momentum in the years leading up to the war.

For this reason too, then, Appelfeld cannot be defined as a Holocaust writer in the direct sense. Katerina is not in this novel a victim of it herself, and, since she is in prison, she is not even, literally, an observer. But she does dwell on the borders of Jewish identity, and is a victim of the horror as well as a witness to the ongoing hatred and murder that was to culminate in ultimate eradication. The testimony of the narrative is to a permanent situation of which the Holocaust is a part, albeit a part in its most extreme expression.

For Katerina, the martyred little Benjamin is the true Jesus. He has been Christianised, and Jesus has been Judaised. Her identity has been adulterated, and so her story conveyed from an odd angle. Her evidence gains in authenticity from her status as outsider, whilst it is dependent for its reliability on her insider familiarity. She is one of the author's leading female characters; but unlike Tsili, Bertha and Kitty (leading female characters in other Appelfeld stories), she is non-Jewish, intelligent and dynamic (she takes the initiative). The model of this heroine type is adopted again in *Until the Dawn's Light*. The time span covered in this novel is extensive, and takes in the Holocaust period and beyond. During the "terrible years of the 40s" (114), she could write almost nothing, and what she wrote she destroyed. For the other inmates, this is the occasion for much rejoicing, and so we see that the Holocaust was not a unique event for them, but rather the culmination of an historical process. Again, Katerina is a witness, but a witness at some remove, indirect. She bears testimony through the diseases that she receives on her own body, suffering in self-imposed isolation. The climax was a world without Jews. Then came the emptying of the prisons, and Katerina can wander off. She had been in prison for over forty years by her own account, which conveys some notion of the time scale of the novel, and of the huge span covered within some thirty pages. She is in the countryside in a strange Jew-free world. So she decides to live in the past, which she can achieve through her memoir, reliving her adopted family and the festivals, the rhythm of the year. And then she returns to the village of her birth to complete her own life cycle and to be reunited with those who have gone.

Witness to What?

It seems that there can be no simple answer to the question of whether Appelfeld is a Holocaust writer. In part, the reason is glaringly obvious; it depends what we mean by the term in question. But it is also because the narratives do lend themselves to be seen as an investigation into the Jewish condition, one of tribal fragility and exposure, that culminated in the full horror of virtual and calculated extinction. On the other hand, there is no direct portrayal of the process of mass murder itself, in fact, hardly even a direct mention, although the awareness is either assumed or filtered indirectly. Perhaps this is not surprising in the light of what is taken to be Appelfeld's *ars poetica*, his belief that all true spiritual concerns should be filtered through personal experience.[11] The personal experience of the survivor, the hunted, the involved observer, forms the content of the narrative, and also connects with the earlier and collective experience of the tribe. The narrative is most convincing and persuasive when the story holds sway, free of overt authorial intervention and comment. It is least successful when succumbing to static metaphorisation and omniscient manipulation. The characters of the story can take over. It is their personal experience that creates the vital force of the narrative, and it is the linkage of that individual experience with the collective that can render a larger meaning and make the story worth conveying. In historical terms, the individual pieces of evidence belong to a pathetically small band of survivors, as against the vast numbers of those perished and rendered necessarily inarticulate. But, for the individual, it is his own experience that counts (recounts, tells).

In the story, "Bagovah haqar" (On the Cold Heights),[12] a few survivors of the war are gathered together, at the instigation of the well-meaning allies, at a beautiful but remote spot in Southern Italy, because "[...]they thought that this far off location, with the virtues of beauty and height, can serve as a creative gangway back into life" (136). The collective story, it is decided too, has to be written up. A "narrator" is appointed, but this narrator has difficulty in arriving at the necessary judgements. Generalisations, it seems, cannot be admitted; presumably, they are invalid. But further: "What right has he to tell the story of this community?" The whole notion of the act of

---

[11] See the author's statement in *Masot beguf rishon* and the development of the notion in the critical work by Lily Rattok, *Bayit al belimah: omanut hasipur shel a. apelfeld* (A Precarious House: The Narrative Art of A.Appelfeld). Heqer. Tel Aviv, 1989.

[12] Included in the volume, *Bagay haporeh*. In the Fruitful Valley. Schocken. Tel Aviv, 1963.

writing in this context becomes problematic and suspect. And, of course, this is precisely the activity that the author is engaged upon in this project and, for that matter, in his total opus. It is for this reason that Rattok regards this as a "key story" in Appelfeld's opus; it opens up the question of the function and capacity of the Holocaust writer.[13] It becomes clear that it is not sufficient merely to describe the events, although that in itself may be extremely difficult, but one must strive for some sort of meaning. On the one hand, the "narrator" fails in his appointed mission. But, on the other, his success is indicated by the existence of the text before us. So it looks as though the effort in itself constitutes the achievement. As Rattok says, the story tells us about a story that was not written.

As far as the narrator invoked in the story is concerned, the narratives must remain within him, where they will have their own life like fireworks (143). "The redemptive word did not appear" (148). The narrator in fact comes to terms with his own incapacity, his inability to transform the experience into words, and recognises the fact that other forces are operative here, and they will take over, imposing their own rule. That, in effect, is what happens. The remnants of the tribe move on, and so ends the story. The Italian episode has acted as an intermediary stage between the world of the camps and the life that awaits, whatever that may be. In parallel fashion, the narrator's function is to mediate between the experience of the survivors and the reality of the reader. Although, he himself may negate the possibility of that function, the ambition to represent the situation faithfully remains in itself the achievement of that mediation. That is all that can be done at this stage, in view of the damage inflicted on the human capacity of characters involved. The implication is that any suggestion of immediately effective and adequate narrative would be facile, and thus do violence to the truth of what has taken place.

Do we know how long this intermediate stage is to endure? On the way from one situation to another, it may well be that, in terms of the ongoing Appelfeld narrative, we are still in the transition stage. The Israeli settings of the opus are nugatory, and, such as they are,

---

[13] See Lily Rattok, op. cit. p.11 & c.

they represent the figures from this European world in settings frozen in postures derived from the past. And his most recent work too does not enter more into the world of specifically current Israeli concerns, but more frequently goes further back, behind the Holocaust and to the sense of modern Jewry on the verge of disintegration following the stages of partial emancipation.

Appelfeld has rejected the label "Holocaust writer", which is so often applied to him.[14] He argues that only about one third of his work deals directly with the subject. This may indeed be the case in a literal sense. A great deal of his work, as we have indicated here, is set in earlier periods, before the rise of Hitler. And some of his narratives are placed in post-war Palestine and Israel. But the earlier settings cast the Jew in the role of failed assimilationist, inauthentic Christian, would-be European. They could have been written in the light of hindsight, with the prevision of ultimate disaster. The post-Holocaust stories, too, are preoccupied with the survivors, remnants of the tribe, a pathetic band of isolated and marginal individuals who gradually form something of a group in the shadow of a larger society. It is in this sense that we see Appelfeld as a "Holocaust writer", a category that must be qualified, refined and individualised to take in his very specific narrative mould.

---

[14] See the reference to the interview in the *New York Times Book Review*, November 15, 1986 in Gila Ramras-Rauch, *Aharon Appelfeld: The Holocaust and Beyond*. Indiana University Press. Bloomington and Indianapolis, 1994. p.18.

VI

FILL THAT GAP:
THE SPACE SAGE, YOEL HOFFMANN

Israeli Fiction

Whatever the external form of mainstream twentieth century Hebrew prose over the course of its colourful history, it has predominantly reflected an Israeli (and previously, Palestinian) social reality. We see this in the recent cases, for example, of Yaakov Shabtai (1934-1981) and David Grossman (b. 1954), whose fiction, although innovative and experimental, has produced a familiar and transparent portrait of the society from which it has emerged. Both have constructed a realistic picture of Tel Aviv, as a city, with its sights, smells and the characters who populate it. These examples could be multiplied a dozen times in any survey of the principal directions of Israeli fiction, which is most commonly rooted in, and stems from, the earth of a recognisable locus.

This is not the case with the minimalist writing of Yoel Hoffmann (b.1937). Hoffmann has been producing enigmatic and suggestive prose fictions in Hebrew for the last ten years or so. In these sparse texts and anti-texts, the effects suggested derive from the words written down, so that the form becomes integral to the matter, and the two act together. Nevertheless, the central characters of these stories are similarly situated as isolated figures in an alien environment that has to be studied and interpreted. The texts themselves progress from straightforward and conventional narratives to sparser, sometimes even single paragraphs that distance themselves from the pages around. We observe this in the figures of the child, Kätschen, in the first of the volumes and in the adult, Bernhard, of the second. The observable difference between the two is not only of that between a child's view of the world and an adult view, but also between two views of language. One can be regarded as naïve, accepting it on its surface value, and identifying the object with the verbal indicator, i.e. the word that describes it, and the other is analytical, quizzical, casting doubt on this presumed identification.[1]

The Book of Joseph

Hoffmann's earliest book is a collection of four novellas.[2] The first of the stories, "Kätschen", introduces the eponymous hero as little boy, observer, companion to his Uncle Arthur, newly arrived in Palestine.[3] The narrative is continuous, and invites the reader to see the world from the child's point of view. He is surrounded by adults, and the key distinction that he makes between them is as between the '*krank*' and the '*nicht krank*' (the sick and the healthy). He had learnt that his father had belonged to the former category, was institutionalised, and then died. So this becomes a crucial distinction, a key to understanding the world. The introduction of the child into the world is his induction into the world of old people who get progressively weaker until they disappear. The distinction drawn between his uncle and his father is based on the observation that the uncle could stand up to the "schon wieder" (again already) that has attacked him better than could his father. But this "schon wieder" eventually weakens and defeats his uncle too. Thus is confirmed the child's perception of the world through concrete images, imperfectly imprinted on the

---

1. There is a discussion of this issue in Hanna Herzig, *Hashem haperati: masot al yaakov shabtai, yehoshua kenaz, yoel hofman*. Hakibbutz Hameuchad. Tel Aviv, 1994: '[T]he dominant thrust in all Hoffmann's works is the joining of the wild and unexpected with the simple and pure into something that could not be said otherwise.' p.104.
2. Yoel Hoffmann, *Sefer yosef* (The Book of Joseph). Keter. Jerusalem, 1988. Second printing, 1991, edition cited here.
3. The child's life corresponds closely to Hoffmann's own. The author himself was taken to Palestine from Hungary in 1938, when just one year old.

child's mind and transformed in his imagination. The little boy is not only exclusively confined to the company of the old, but to the very old, those nearing death. He lacks the company both of his parents, now deceased, and of people of his parents' age, but also of his own contemporaries, as Uncle Arthur had taken him away from school for teaching him such rubbish ("Unsinn", i.e. nonsense, which Kätschen understands as "Ameisen", i.e. ants.) Uncle Arthur and his Hungarian friend Max plan to teach the child at home, as he is particularly gifted, and so they confide to his Aunt Oppenheim, who has the primary responsibility for his upbringing. So the little boy is regarded as a sort of prince, and comes in for a very specially protected place in the scheme of things and the world around. It is a protected place, but a very lonely one too, deprived of normal company, speaking a language foreign to his environment, and thus alienated from his immediate circumstances.

It is difficult to distinguish between dream world and reality in this story. Although the narrative is conveyed in the third person, the centre of consciousness is that of the little boy, a child trying to make sense of his environment, and, in doing so, imposing his view on puzzling and even contradictory elements. Thus, he obtains some sense of harmony. The child seems to be hurled into a world without primary and natural parental support, although all the other adults around fight to take the child under their wing. But, it seems, for reasons that are not spelled out, that Kätschen has to go to a kibbutz. However, this new home seeks to deprive the little boy of his current identity, his name and his language. But the little boy insists on his own, original name, even if he can only make that point to a cow (29). The child observes that the principal activity of the kibbutz seems to be "cutting", and so, metaphorically, they have cut the "Herr" from Herr Grossman (secretary of the kibbutz), and they would cut out his own identity too. In his unconscious flight from his new, alien environment, he associates every new experience and each new acquaintance with his old family. Thus the old Arab who comes to his rescue, following his straying outside the territory, is seen as 'a sort of Uncle Arthur' (32), sometimes speaking the same language (presumably a projection) and sometimes a strange language, an Arabic that sounds very pleasant to him. It is clear that there had been some opposition, at least on the part of the old friend Max, to this disposal of the child. Max had not been a Zionist, but a believer in "Music", "the Zionism of people" rather than just of Jews (22).

The experiences of other, older people, those with mysterious past lives are represented by half phrases, and the child constructs his own world picture. The cow has become his familiar, but has now gone away. The story concludes with the child united once more with his father. But there is a question in the child's mind as to whether the father, who is a sort of prophet, knowing the past and the future, can discern the actuality before his eyes, i.e. the present. They wander off to a market, and the child imagines first that by exercising magical powers,he can freeze the situation and have it permanently. But that was all nonsense (48). Now they can wander off, out of the market, out of the town, and into the fields. Now too, looking into his father's eyes, he can ask him the critical question: "'Do you know who I am?'"[4] To which he receives the confirming answer: "' Yes. Kätschen.'" (49)

This is a puzzling story, dreamlike, childlike, but with strands of the reality of a strange environment and an estranged child perceiving and observing. Pieces of biography and autobiography compose the enigmatic tales of Hoffmann. The title story of this volume likewise details a chronology. The eponymous hero flees from Russia to Berlin with his child, following the Cossack murder of his beloved wife in 1928, and settles in Alexander Platz, where the non-German Jews were reputed to be living. He refuses to call his child by a proper name, but only by the generic "yingele" so as to perpetuate the memory of his late wife, who had so addressed him. In the meantime, a parallel story develops around one Siegfried and his lust after Brünhilde. The narrative proceeds chronologically through to 1933, the year that "Gornicht", Joseph's assistant, who had befriended Yingele, goes to London in pursuit of an English lady, who turns out to be the daughter of his compatriot, Froika Goldstein, now in a successful tailoring business. Gornicht joins them in the business as son-in-law and partner. He has now made it.

---

4. All translations here are my own - LIY.

The complexity of the plot and the multiplicity of the characters create the necessity of a complex, multi-tiered narrative confined within the space of a novella. The comic dimensions and the international sweep do not sit easily with the awesome implications of time, space and situation, viz. that of the Jews landed in Berlin after 1933. The strands have to be drawn together. There are other elements in the story as well, which the narrator, in the manner of eighteenth century novelists, also does not want to let us forget. There is, for example, the brother of Gornicht, who has remained in Hungary. For Yingele and Joseph in Berlin, times get harder. Yingele has to stay at home now in fear. But although for the Germans, the figure of his father, Joseph, is diminished, for the son, it expands. It is the image, the epigram that makes the familiar story concrete, and clothes it with specific and characteristic dress of Joseph's story. Joseph assumes gigantic dimensions, becomes an oak tree in the child's dream, a source of power from which everything else takes its sustenance. But being a source of food for others also takes its toll on the stock as it gets eaten away. The story can assume mythical proportions. Yingele, under the oppressive waves of the present circumstances, tries desperately to rid himself of his own image, that is to say, to get away from his own self. Perhaps then he can be of "fair countenance" like the others around. The image in the mirror, however, obstinately clings to him despite all his efforts; he is condemned to stay with himself, untransformed: 'How can I be other than what I am, thinks Yingele, and is filled with sadness.' (94)

The two plots, one relating to Siegfried (the archetypally German name) and the one relating to Joseph and Yingele, come together in the fateful year, 1938. Siegfried happens upon Yingele, and cracks open his skull. At the sight of this, Joseph's heart is broken. Following the expanse of "purification", Germany becomes clear as crystal (109),[5] as the shattered glass reflects the dislocation of the Jews from the body politic. The text moves into a prose with broken lines of metreless and rhymeless poetry. The separate lines, often in themselves sentences, indicate discrete subjects and activities, suggesting highly variegated content and a life of variety, as

---

5. An obvious reference to *Kristallnacht*, taking place on November 9-10, 1938.

emerging in the story. The scene thereafter moves back to Gornicht and London. And the aftermath of the war takes him back to Berlin in search of the traces of Joseph and Yingele. But of course, they are no longer to be found, and in a world without the two of them, he can no longer function (121). In despair, he accepts the offer of sex in a bar, and, in the course of consummation, shrieks out the *kaddish*, thus bringing lust into line with death.

How to tell a story

In one of his stories,[6] the author both relates a plot with its characters and development and self-consciously meditates on the art of fiction, what has to be there, and the difficulties of fictional contrivance. The problem is a sort of catch. In order to present the characters truly, in all their complexity and significance, a great deal of exposition has to be offered; origins, situation, development etc. But coversely, once this has been done, the reader's attention has been lost, and a good deal of material not relevant to the skeletal structure of the selected narrative has been heaped up. There is no better way to demonstrate this than by telling the story of Ursula and Gustav, or, at least, by trying to tell the story of Ursula and Gustav. You start to tell it, and, in the telling, have to clarify and explain, otherwise, it makes no sense. But, once you have done that, it is difficult to get back to the main point. But the telling of this in itself becomes part of the story: 'This discussion has gone on for too long, and the reader is partly to blame. It is not reasonable to expect the writer to parade before his readers every episode that comes up incidentally, and to delve into it until it becomes totally clear. The events that are central to our concern are, obviously, the birth of Ursula and Gustav.' (129) You can not sensibly exhaust each topic before proceeding to the next, otherwise there would be no end to it. This witty investigation is accompanied by a string of examples, not only of the possibilities

---

6. "Ben harim uvein slaim tasah harakevet" in *Sefer yosef. Texte*. Éditions du Seuil. Paris, 1973. P. 19.
6. Yoel Hoffmann, *Christus shel dagim* (Christ of Fish). Keter. Jerusalem, 1991.

that were actualised in the plot, but also, to be true to the nature of the characters, of those that were not.

Another way of formulating the problem is to say that the figures in a narrative can only function in a context too large for the writer's vision. There is no writer whose breadth of vision is such that he can embrace everything happens at the time that the action of his story is taking place. This is the function of the reader; he has to fill in the space of the text before him with what is not before him. The mind of the reader is situated in a context much broader than would be constrained by the bounds of the immediate text. The writer, on the other hand, leaves a space, and it is that space that becomes significant. For example, in the Jesus story by the Gospel writers, it is precisely the shadowy figure of the carpenter Joseph who is interesting; the reader can not but dwell on his everyday activities, which are not mentioned specifically in the texts. 'The greatness of Joseph the carpenter, husband of the holy Mary, lies not in what the story attributes to him, but in what it does not attribute to him. (133).

There is another issue too. If something happens, it is inevitable, so the thing is hardly worth the telling. This the author finds unbearable, but he still has to carry out his function of description, otherwise his story would not move forward. (139) Perhaps the answer lies in offering a very terse and economical précis, so that the reader too knows where he stands, and that the words are just there out of necessity. A writer too uses the language of analogy in order to clarify his point, but then, firstly, the analogy is never totally appropriate and demands constant reworking, and then, the analogical figure might divert the reader's attention and take over centre stage. By the time the issue has been clarified, and it is decided why it was adopted, the original point of the story has been forgotten.

In the actual story, the one being related by the author on the page before us, the author feels that he must return to the main plot. But the plot is not without explication and commentary. This is all to get back to the hero and heroine, who themselves can only be situated through the prior positioning of their parents. This is all told, naturally enough, for the reader, or, at any rate, for a reader. How does such a reader react? For example, the author's wife? '"This story does not develop at all, but goes on twisting itself like a snail", said the author's wife, putting on her earrings.' (152) But, in fact, it seems that the story had not been controlled by the author, but had written itself. The author has to explain what he has found, and only has a right to reject what he himself had forged with his own intention.

Hoffmann's stories, then, are exercises in text and super text, text and commentary, matter and explication. The secondary ledge of the material becomes an integrated part of the whole. The reader too is involved, and may too slide into the narrative, as we have seen in the case of the author's wife. Plot has merged into background, submerged by intention, capped by device, observed from the outside, recapitulated, and then followed through. In the final story of the volume here, "Curriculum Vitae", the author returns to present an account of himself. But this too moves on to the accidents of his life, his parents, his teachers and his first loves. It seems to be very hard to delimit oneself in a story, and this tendency then becomes the actual story.

Bernhard

The novel, *Bernhard* (Bernhard, 1989), the author's first long fiction, sets the tone. It is broken up into paragraphs, each normally occupying a page of text, which, in its turn, is then followed by a blank page. But it may be that these intersteces are the most alluring points. Roland Barthes writes, comparing the text to an erotic experience: 'L'endroit le plus érotique d'un corps n'est il pas *là où le vêtement bâille*?' (The most erotic part of the body is where there is a gap in the clothing.)[7] What looks like a paradox, that what is not there is the most vital element, is contingent on what precedes and what follows.

Bernhard links himself to space, as he does to his recently deceased wife. He ponders how material essence, infinite and all containing space, can create a separate and unique individual, himself for example. The death of his wife, Paula, leads him to a preoccupa-

---

7. Roland Barthes, *Le Plaisir du Texte*. Éditions du Seuil. Paris, 1973. P. 19.

tion with the revelation of truth (giluy haemet, p.5). Since space contains all, including all tenses; past, present and future, he tries to form a picture of it exclusive of himself, his own subjectivity. But he is always there at the margins of that picture (p. 7).

The novels are an expression of speculative philosophy, so they cannot be removed from its form. Form is also the content. Such novels, here specifically, *Bernhard*, are composed of epigrammatic propositions, pithy statements, perfectly rounded. The model for these statements is clearly Spinoza. But here, they take on the guise of fiction. They relate to abstract and permanent truths, but are also located in time and constructed by the narrator, so do not escape his intervention and shaping. The narrative voice remains inseparable from the text, allowing a space for construction and observation beyond. Unlike speculative philosophy, these fictions are related to specific incidents in time, and themselves relate to individuals and their "accidents". The philosophical problem is the relationship of the universal to the particular. Philosophy deals with the former; it applies at all times and in every place, without regard to the specific. Fiction deals with the latter, and is precisely concerned with a given moment as lived in by a particular, as well as changing, person, governed by accretions of detail. Bernhard reflects that, as Spinoza said, because we observe only the external accidents, we imagine that things actually happen. But the reality, i.e. God's reality, is permanent, because unchanging (p. 8). All discourse, which is necessarily human and therefore contingent, has to be subjected to the perspective of the external which is eternal. Bernhard's difficulty is to retain this dual perspective, to see the permanent through the transient, whilst also observing his own transience and necessarily partial view.

What and who is Bernhard? Bernhard is living in the twentieth century, is of German extraction and background, and emigrates to Palestine/Israel, whilst retaining a strong German accent and speech habits. But in Israel too, he is pursued by transient sensations whilst also appreciating that they are, in the final analysis, insignificant. Or, are they? Does it not rather depend on who is doing the seeing? Is it God, or just the pathetic individual through his decrepit organs? This man, exiled from his natural home, sees himself as disembodied: 'His feet paddling in water and his head in the mist. He is without baggage. He is a limitless Bernhard. People pass him by as though in a mirror' (p. 17). This is a tale of Bernard's absorption into his adopted Land of Israel. But the background narrative movement is punctuated by reports of Hitler's conquests in Europe.

D.S. Gregory, Bernhard's fictional creation, meanwhile yearns for "data", for something to happen, and to be able to make an impression on the world around, that is, to affect the environment in which he finds himself. The expression of his erotic life comes through romantic fantasy; "the flapping of butterfly wings...the holy Trinity" (p. 60), but this is contrasted with grey reality; "the thousands of Hungarian cutting their toenails." (ibid.) There are always, it seems, two plains of activity, and thus two plains of reality, and this is what makes life so difficult to absorb and to comprehend as a totality. Gregory is the hero of Bernhard's novel (p. 23). But the author cannot, in his own perception, decide his character's future, nor can he really distinguish between the feelings of his creation and his own. The experiences that he ascribes to Gregory are in effect Bernhard's. (p. 42) But, they seem to emerge as though from Gregory's own imagination, as though he is creating his own novel, and then living in it (p. 60). Gradually, through these ellipses, a series of characters emerges, some dependent on each other, and some the product of each other; Bernhard, his late wife, Paula, (whom he still fantasises), Gustav, Herzog, Gregory, his mother, Yakterina, and his lover, Isabella, Benvenisti and Elvira. There is also Bernhard's late father, Sigmund, who died in 1920. His mother, Clara, had also died, but the basis of sadness for him lay in another death, more remote, that of one 'old Kovacs', who had tried, obviously unsuccessfully, to stop a train in its tracks. That was "the first sorrow" (p. 125) in a chain of sorrows that mark out his life. Now, the father Sigmund's spirit assumes the form of a headscarf, and we must wonder whether that spirit still hovers over the son in Palestine, as it did in Berlin (p. 118).

But the difficulty experienced by the novel's focus of reference, Bernhard, is the reality of separate individuals, and the space between them. What is the difference, for example, between talking about someone one's foot and that person's shoelace? And if you can distinguish between the person's foot and the person himself, up to what point can you remove the possessor of the foot from the essence of the person? In other words, if you can ascribe possession to a possessor in regard to his body, where is the possessor beyond the body? Another question that preoccupies Bernhard is whether what happens has to happen, or whether circumstances could grant that something else takes its place. He comes to the conclusion, following the pleasurable experience of eating *kefir*, that perhaps an alternative path could have been found; 'Things happen by chance, but they do not happen in any other way.' (p. 69) Perhaps things could have been otherwise in other circumstances. But the reality is that they are not.

The pain that Bernhard feels at the loss of his wife, Paula, is, for him, more real than it could be if he were a fictional figure (p. 70). Perhaps this then is the difference between fantasy and reality, the difference between sensation and imagination. This, however, is only a distinction that can be perceived subjectively. In the meantime, the war progresses to its historical conclusion; external and internal reality move in lines not quite parallel. Public events and the specific story of Bernhard both come to their conclusion at the same time in the novel. Not dissimilarly, our hero ponders Descartes' view that, though flesh and spirit are both created by God, they move along on separate lines, like two clocks, one striking when the other points to the appropriate hour (p. 156). The two are interdependent; soul without space, and body without soul. They derive their movement from each other, but, in this, they are independent of God, after having received their initial impulse from Him.

Seeing a performance of *Hamlet*, together with Gustav, at the end of the war, Bernhard connects the promise of Fortinbras, who enters a stage cluttered with corpses, heralding a new world. Bernhard extrapolates that there could be a new world here too (p. 169). It all depends on whether there is another world. Gustav is imaged: 'suspended in space, above the roofs of Rehavia.' (p. 174) The conclusion is pregnant with possibilities; the crucified figure looks at his mother, the virgin Mary, and says: "See a woman, behold thy son. Bernhard then gives birth to a new child. Here there is another reality, that of Gustav in Jerusalem, in whose kitchen our hero is sitting, listening to Bach's *St. John's Passion*.

The Christ of Fish

This episodic memoir from childhood[8] is even more eccentric in form. Like his first volume, this book attempts to enter the world of childhood, and adopt a childlike perspective. But, as we can see from the use of tenses and time scales, there is an adult voice mediating between the present narrative self and that distant child, into whose persona he projects backwards by recollection. What we glean both of the current narrator and of that child is achieved through the suggestive text, what is in it as well as what is omitted. The school composition that he tells us about reveals a specific perspective which draws criticism from his teacher (para 4). The subject is, "What One Sees in the Market". He writes about a mongoloid man, staring at a vat full of fish all day. The teacher noted on the composition that he should have written about 'everything that one sees.' The author has already adopted a selective vision, and chosen to dwell on that, in the view of others perhaps, to the detriment of a broader, all encompassing overview.

However, unlike the "Joseph" collection, this book seems to defy generic categorisation. In the vein of an ancient work, the text is broken up into many short sections, here 233 in number, including illustrations and exemplifications. There is a narrative link, held together by the first person narrator, and the now accepted gap is left on alternate pages. Again, the reader is required, if he so wishes, to make good the lack. Or perhaps, he can simply meditate on the blank spaces that provide a relief from the dense content.

The tales of Hoffmann seem to veer from the random and trivial to the deeply significant within a very short space. He even presents the obvious question to himself: 'Why am I relating all these things?' (para. 7), to which the answer given is: 'As I carry on relating, I shall one day know (without thinking about it) what the most beautiful thing in the world is. And when I do know I shall say; "This thing (whatever it is) is the most beautiful thing in the world."' That seems to be something worth striving for. The narrative also considers the results of speculation and concentration. What can be achieved by

---

8. Yoel Hoffmann, Christus shel dagim (Christ of Fish). Keter. Jerusalem, 1991.

these mental activities? What is death, and how can it be imaged? It must be possible to acquire knowledge he realises, as he knows, for example, that he has learnt some Sanskrit words from his uncle. But that seems an implausible psychic movement (para. 13). The existence of the world can be both asserted and doubted on one and the same basis, by his brilliant Uncle Herbert (para. 28). The narrator, though, is potentially drawn to total scepticism in the quest for his personal identity. He wants to know whether his own experiences, as perceived by his subjectivity, are authentically his own. Perhaps they are rather the dream of some other person (para. 37). Another character, who posits a useful world view is Paul, another person of German origin living in Tel Aviv, and a close friend of his Aunt Magda, a character summarily introduced. That man's aspiration is spiritual, but it is to be modified by the rational element, as in the philosophy of his new model, Moses Mendelssohn. This rational element boosts the power of spiritual life (paras. 38, 39), and still ensures eternity beyond matter (para. 40). That unrelated facts coexist, and possibly have no effect on each other is constantly noted. Perhaps this is an occasion for surprise, certainly for comment, as we might expect the facets of all universal existence to be interconnected, and, therefore, mutually influential. In the child's mind, classical elements invade the present day, pieces of German poetry come into the classroom (Schiller's poem is associated with the vice principal of the school, para. 53), when the Garden of Eden is invoked. Fragments of words and detached dialogue filter through to the child's consciousness, and are duly reassembled here in these paragraphs. Paul and Magda seem to have concourse with a reality beyond what is immediately experienced.

What then looks like a collection of discrete units becomes the fragmented memoir of childhood. At a slightly later stage, presumably coinciding with the author's own recollection of adolescence, the narrator's memoir slows down, and gains more particularity and adult-like realism. From fragments, we move to chronological sequence. The atmosphere also changes, as we shift into post-mandatory Palestine. But the images still possess grotesque shapes. On a journey in the Haifa region: 'Mount Carmel distanced itself from Paul's head, backwards.' (para. 65) So, it looks as though the landscape is moving, rather than the train. There seems to be an implied family crisis when Paul marries someone called Edna, and Aunt Magda adopts the habit of going to the Café Pilz. She has to acclimatise herself to Paul's absence and to life without him. The narrator speculates as to whether things would work out differently if this account were fictional, a novel, rather than factual (para. 79). So the reader is brought up against a contrast; an assumption of historicity within the framework of a strangely built novel.

There is a conscious awareness of the limitations of narratorial authority. The first person narrator writes that he wants to talk about a certain Mr. Moskovic, and in order to do this adequately, he must know sufficient about him and his circumstances to place him in the narrative. But before one can do this (properly and truly?), one should know everything about him. Otherwise, the picture presented will be distorted or partial, at any rate, imperfect (para. 83). The rest is speculation, and in the following paragraph, there is only a 'maybe' relating to him. Similarly, in the account of André (another character introduced without preamble), questions are raised but decisive answers not offered (para. 124). The book, in its progression, becomes more of a consecutive narrative, relating the stories of Aunt Magda and André, describing their changing circumstances and the process of aging. We have a certain degree of biography, followed by speculation. When did this old lady, Magda, first know love, for example? (para. 167) But the narrative moves backwards as well as forward. For example, it goes back to the 50s and to Paul's romantic attention, as expressed in the bottle that he brought to her (para. 174).

Part of the process of life, and indeed its necessary climax, is death. Death is a process of consciousness not an experience, as death is nothing: 'Death may indeed be nothing in itself, yet the consciousness of death is in most cultures very much a part of life.'[9] This was written with particular reference to Japanese culture, but, as the words themselves indicate, it applies universally. In this novel, it is Mr. Moskovic's move towards death that is charted. In comparing

---

9. See Yoel Hoffmann's preface to his own book, *Japanese Death Poems*. Charles E. Tuttle Company. Tokyo, 1986, p.9.

David Hume's thought to Buddhist philosophy, Hoffmann notes Hume's stress on sensations, which are divided into two categories. We experience these sensations '[e]xternally, in the case of stimulation through the five senses; or internally, either through the appearance of feelings and desires, or as faint recollections.'[10] Mr. Moskovic has '[h]is hair growing inwards, into his body. This was the external sign of disorder in the directions of time' (para. 194). And this is the closest possible verbal approximation to the sensation of that consciousness. Hermina's death is also described, but this from the outside. Is her body light (although apparently heavy), or is her spirit light? (para. 201) Aunt Magda's loss of sight, sudden as it is, is first articulated (she says; "'I cannot see'", para. 229), and then represented by black shapes intervening in the text. Suddenly too, through her blindness, she manages to see the soul of everything: 'And she knew (Oh, how she knew!) that this world carries into the next world just as it is. Without distinction. And all directions are reversed.' (para. 233) This is how the novel ends, with an assertion through Aunt Magda, that finally, all is a unity, life, death, past and future.

How are you, Dolores?

A more recent novel, *Mah shlomekh dolores* (How are You, Dolores? 1995), adds to the now familiar typesetting devices, the paragraphing and the printing on alternate pages, the unusual, and very costly, factor of pointed Hebrew. A further feature is the now familiar use of photographs within the text, accepted now in contemporary literature. Here we have the appearance of a buxom lady in various states of undress; or rather, alternately dressed and undressed. The black and white, of the rather old fashioned reproductions, looms from the printed word, attracting the reader's attention, and alerting him to further implications. What is contributed by these elements, and how do they function in the fiction? One

---

10. Yoel Hoffmann, *The Idea of Self - East and West*. Firma KLM Private Limited. Calcutta, 1980, p.2.

way in which they have to function is to slow down the reading pace, and then concentrate the mind as though the reader is coping with a holy text.[11] It is also built up mathematically, and there is a prevalent concern with numbers. The whole novel consists of 3 books, each of which contains 111 units. But also, we have the main character assuming the narrational role, thus becoming the focus of consciousness, and she (the narrator is female) seems to take up where Aunt Magda left us in *The Christ of Fish,* flying in the air. She conducts would be dialogues, but there is no-one at the other end.: 'I cry out (an internal cry) Dolores Dolores as though I have a friend of that name./ How are you Dolores (I say to myself) and exchange recipes for dresses with her'. (para. 34). Multiplicity is contained within the single unit, as with the "raven", so suggestive of foreboding: 'I love your rich language. This one word of yours which has all the constructions.' (para. 43). The narrator's only contact seems to be with Dolores, whom she addresses constantly. Her concerns are metaphysical, and like Hume,[12] she raises the issue of how a point can exist without extension (para. 65). Can there be something which both exists and does not exist? After all, a point has to be represented, and therefore has substance and extension so that we can see it. On the other hand, it is a theoretical entity, and its function is precisely to have no substance. Paradoxically, the book itself becomes an iconic object, with its strange and distancing typesetting, paragraphing, pagination and photographs. They do not illustrate the text as much as to provide an analogue. They do not share the same necessary tendency as the sound and sense of the printed words. It is these words that are abbreviated, allusive and elliptical.

The second book raises the issue of identity; only a thing which is different from itself can be articulated, and this can never be the

---

11. It is primarily the Biblical text that is pointed. In fact the pointing system was invented by the massoretes for the accurate rendering and interpretation of the holy material.

12. David Hume, *A Treatise of Human Nature.* ed. L.A.Selby-Bigge. Oxford University Press. Oxford, 1888, reprinted 1968, p.44, Book 1, Section IV. Hume deals with the issue of whether a point has extension. In his own view, he offers '[a] clear proof, that the ideas of surfaces, lines and points admit not of any division; those of surfaces in depth; of lines in breadth and depth; and of points in any dimension.'.

case (para. 115). However, there is another paradox, and it is particularly relevant to the function of artistic activity. This is to fill in the space between objects; the sort of thing that Van Gogh achieved in his painting. He managed to draw the wind, a non visible entity, the space between the trees (para. 117). Is it perhaps reasonable to posit that the narrator here regards that as akin to her own function, which, by implication, is what literature can also manage. She says: 'What others cut I bleed, as though I am a cake or cloth' (para. 119). What we have to learn, she asserts, is (and it is her own secret garnered from the cats, with which she associates): 'the thoughts within the empty spaces' (para. 123). The artist holds certain truths, as one aware of the materially imperceptible, a very present reality, but one linked by quantum connections to sources above. The hustle and bustle of Tel Aviv life serves as a metaphor for the connection between lower and upper strata of existence, and the narrator hands over what she receives to Dolores.

There is constantly pointed out the apparently random but necessary intersection between the superficial specific and the imponderably mysterious. All of this amounts to, no less, the question of the meaning of life, particularly that of personal identity: '[h]uman language vis-à-vis its implausibility, particularly the words this and I' (para. 165). In the third "book", the narrator addresses a male, whom she calls Michael, and speaks of her new child. But Michael is also addressed as her child. So that child could be the second person, the addressee, in the book.

The apparent randomness, the disconnected nature of the work, is paralleled by the portrait of Japanese poetry as transmitted by Hoffmann.[13] Types of poetry, as well as different styles and periods are presented within a single volume. But, in addition, much of the poetry described and quoted is characterised by the *haiku* tradition of "saying something without saying it".[14] The *haiku* (seventeen syllables, with three lines, of which the middle one is the longest) is the shortest verse form that exists, and is therefore characterised by its ultimate distillation, striving for condensation of external, compound

---

13. Yoel Hoffmann ed. with introduction and commentary, *Japanese Death Poems*.
14. Ibid. p.24.

elements: '*Haiku* poetry resounds with endless meanings just because it so often attains that perfect simplicity sought for in philosophy, religion, literature, and art.'[15] The Hoffmann narratives likewise strive for this distillation. But they allow for the reader's interpretation, response and intervention, whilst remaining discreetly silent beyond the first cryptic statement. The factual statement is left hanging, without explication or comment. The last "word" is of course not one word at all, but the expressionless statement that 'we ate cucumbers on the grass.' In "death poems", it is not only the distillation that is ultimate, but the notions of truth that can transcend conventional forms of politeness and restraint in the straining after the verbal equivalent of final truth.[16] It is not so much the customary form of poetic expression, as '[t]he *spiritual* legacy of the Japanese.'[17] Is there not something of this that serves as a model here for the strange Hebrew fictions of Hoffmann?

15. Ibid. p.25.
16. Ibid. pp.27, 28.
17. Ibid. p.28.

VII

MEMORIALISATION IN NEW FICTION

The Past in the Present

Distinctions between fiction and biography blur. In the literature of the past, the reader was normally aware of the generic nature of the material that was being read. There was little presumed doubt as to whether the thrust was documentary, whether it was a historical and factual account, or whether it was fictional, invented. And, if there was such doubt, this was incorporated into the overall opus, and became integral to the genre. We see this for example in Daniel Defoe's account of the plague year, where the author adopted the pose of a diarist recording the events from an earlier age, but as though writing at the time, experiencing the dreadful spectacle and himself, naturally, under threat.[1] On the other hand, when the

---

1. Daniel Defoe, *A Journal of the Plague Year*. London, 1722. This was initially published in 1722, but presented by the author as though a diary written during the events described, i.e. in the year 1665. Anthony Burgess, in his Introduction to edition of the Penguin English Library, 1966, writes that the work reads as though: '[a] genuine book of memoirs. This is what it reads like and is meant to read like - a rapid, colloquial, sometimes clumsy setting down of reminiscences of a great historical event that was lived through by a plain London merchant with a passion for facts, a certain journalistic talent, but...no literary pretensions whatever.' p.6. The book is signed by "H.F.", presumed to be a man living contemporaneously with the events, perhaps a relative of the author, Henry Foe, who was aged 37 at the time that the plague broke out. Despite the unambiguous "fictionality" of the account, a

assumption of biography or autobiography was made, it was clear that such an assumption served as an agreed convention, either for the purposes of the fiction, or for the establishment of the unadorned fact.

Or so it seemed. But this distinction between historiography representing undiluted facticity, on the one hand, and literariness, the fact including its interpretation and the response of the writer, is itself a fairly modern one. This seems to derive from the ambition to see historiography as an empirical science, stripped of the subjectivity of the historian, on the assumption that a story of the unfolding of events might be told as it "actually" happened. But if we examine the ancient testimonies, the act of interpretation constantly accompanied the fixing of facts. Otherwise, it might have been asked, why tell the story? In the Bible, for example, the events discussed are promulgated together with a confirmation of significance.[2] The point of the narrative text is to confirm and promulgate the kingship of God and His dominion over the events of history. Thus it is, that an apparently convenient dichotomy created between fact and interpretation breaks down in our examination of the actual practice of literature. To put it in another way, matters of fact are also mediated.

A hallmark of the contemporary writer is perhaps the recognition of this unavoidable mediation, followed by narrative qualification. Certainly, one of the characteristics of contemporary writing is the uncertainty created in regard to the borders between the two, between fact and interpretation, either because such divisions are regarded as irrelevant, or in order, deliberately, to allow uncertainty to surface in the mind of the reader. "Crossover" (the term is taken from the current music scene) writing invokes variety and mixture. We may be uncertain in such narrative as to whether we are dealing with an accurate and literal representation of lives and situations, or with an imagined variation on a theme.

---

pseudopigrophon, Burgess calls it '[t]he most reliable and comprehensive account of the Great Plague that we possess.' ibid.

2. For a discussion of this issue see James Young, *Writing and Rewriting the Holocaust: Narrative and the Consequences of Interpretation.* Indiana University Press. Bloomington and Indianapolis, 1988, p. 20-25.

We find an example of this in the novel by the young Israeli writer, Ronit Matalon, *Im hapanim elenu* (Facing Us),[3] where the family background is offered up with a variety of historical commentary, dialogue, and pictorial support. Here, the past is described with such loving detail and passion that these become part of the essence of the novel. An overall picture is created through the dual medium of photographs, or their absence, and a verbal commentary, explicating the visual material with background explication and further amplification.[4] As in a collage, materials from sources other than the pen of the author are imposed on a primary narrative, presumably gaining credence from the duplication of complementary sources.

The story is told by the seventeen year old Esther, who opens with a photo of her uncle, standing with his back to the camera, arms folded, facing his African workers in the Cameroons. This is followed by a detailed analysis of their relative positioning and individual shapes. This sets the tone for the opening of the story which takes place at this uncle, Sicurel's home in Africa, which Esther is visiting at his request. The next chapter, headed by the "missing photo", tells of the uncle's need to reestablish contact with "someone from the family."[5] There is however a "mystery", without which the narrative would no doubt lack tension and substantial interest. This mystery consists of how a member of this Cairene Jewish family, most of whom, including the narrator relocated in Israel, came to settle in this part of Africa. So, the scene is set for a background roundup of how this all happened, with some introduction to the family members, particularly the uncle's siblings, and the dominant role of his brother, Moïse, the single minded Marxist Zionist. We are taken further into a reconstruction of the family history, and how the uncle moved originally to Brazzaville, as

---

3. Ronit Matalon. *Im hapanim elenu*. (Facing Us). Am Oved. Tel Aviv, 1996.
4. It is interesting to understand why this use of the extra medium is seen to be useful. Young comments: 'One of the reasons that narrative and photographs are so convincing together is that they seem to represent a combination of pure object and commentary on the object, each seeming to complete the other by reinforcing a sense of contrasting functions.' See Young, op. cit. pp.57-58.
5. Ibid. p.21.

a "first stop on the black continent".[6] But there is of course one more character here of vital significance in the story, and that is the narrator herself. How did she come to compose the novel, and what was its genesis? The uncle comes into her room to discover her writing a "diary", and he asks her what she is writing about. Her reply is that it is "'about everything happening, what I think, imagine...but chiefly about the present.'"[7] This then is our novel, the record, observation and also the product of the imagination of the narrator. And there is a darker side to this act of record too, as it is, she adds in the explanation offered to her uncle, "'like an inscription on a tombstone.'"[8] The necessary implication that follows then is that we are closing the cover on a book of the past. This is a life that is gone, and the novel here presented is a record of recall. Esther is always writing in her notebook, and it is fair to assume that the material that she notes down constitutes the kernel of the novel before us. The materials for the novel then are the writer's own notes, her recollections, her scrapbooks, and her photographs. In order to reinforce the solid basis of the narrative, there is also added some substantial extracts, interposed from an autobiographical account of the Israeli writer, Jacqueline Kahanoff, who grew up in Cairo. This internationally known author also appears in a photograph together with the narrator's family, taken in Cairo in 1946, and this confirms not only a thematic connection, but a family link too. Kahanoff is concerned with the issue of the minorities there, amongst whom were Jews like herself. It was particularly these minorities who cultivated European education, as well as taking over the position of the ideological opposition. Why does our novel introduce such apparently extraneous material? Well, it seems to broaden the potential base of the fiction, and suggest alternative and refreshing ways of looking at a situation which is not necessarily "fiction", in the sense of unfettered invention. There is a social foundation to Esther's story which cuts in odd directions. The supplementary aids

---

6. Ibid. p.66. See also M.Proust, *Le Temps Retrouvé* in *A la Récherche du Temps Perdu*. Vol 6, Pléiade edition, Paris, p.451, for a presentation of this image of the fictional word as an inscription on a tombstone.
7. Ibid. p.68.
8. Ibid.

are also part of the story, and these are offered thematically rather than chronologically. Presumably, a piece of autobiographical analysis, with its sociological tendency, contributes to the overall understanding of the situation, including the Levantine attitudes of this social sector. A constant contrast is implied between the past and the present. But the starting point is the concrete representation in the photograph, and the novel only arrives at the apparent nub, the manner in which the father got involved with Africa, well over halfway through the text.[9] At this point, she relates of her relative's restlessness, his curiosity, his ambition, which might have collided awkwardly with his pan-Arab sympathies, and his admiration of the Egyptian leader, Nasser. Thus, he landed up in black Africa, still trying to make money. Our narrator attempts a reconstruction of the past, as it involved him, and of his character, through inspection of the image, supported by recollection.

But it is not only the presentation of photographs that comprises a necessary element in the reconstruction of the overall picture. It is also the technique of perusal that must be taken into account. There is an almost infinite multiplicity of materials. But how does one absorb them all? Another relative, the niece Zuza, now living as a journalist in New York and now writing a book about the family's "roots", comes to interview her aunt for information and background to their Cairene life and general awareness. '"In order to see a photograph properly, one must take one's eyes away from it, or just close them," declares Zuza, closing her own eyes, and thrusting her chin forward.'[10] This distancing should presumably put the artefact in context, and enable one to see it more objectively, as the visitor attempts to recapture the family atmosphere in Egypt through the medium of the novel..

For a very different sort of example we may consider the book by the Austro-German writer, now British academic, W.G. Sebald, *The Emigrants*.[11] Here we have a description of four separate people, and their stories, including photographs illustrating their stories.

9. Ibid. p.193.
10. Ibid. p.285.
11. W.G.Sebald. *The Emigrants*. The Harvill Press. London, 1996. Orig. *Die Ausgewanderten*, 1993.

These elements are formed of separate units, but they combine into one rather mournful narrative. In the first account, headed "Dr. Selwyn", Selwyn and his friend Edwin show slides of Switzerland to the narrator: 'I sensed that, for both of them, this return of their past selves was an occasion for some emotion.'[12] But the primary object of Selwyn's longing is the village near Grodno in Lithuania, which he had left at the age of seven. His account relates of his emigration to London (where the family had disembarked, thinking it was New York), and his disguised identity (his surname was changed from Seweryn to Selwyn, for example). The narrator virtually loses contact with Selwyn, but later hears of his suicide: 'And so they are ever returning to us, the dead',[13] this story ends. The cumulative effect of the four accounts gathers strength from the notion of mutual enforcement around a single theme. The emotional charge and implications of the totality assume a knowledge of the historical events that have led to the later and present circumstances. The understatement of the restrained narrative contains all the more power for being implicit. The second account in the book relates of the narrator's primary school teacher who put an end to his life at the age of seventy four, in January 1984. the narrator goes to investigate the case of this Paul Bereyter at the small town of S in the new Germany, and, in so doing, meets up with Lucy Landau, who had been a friend of his, and had also arranged his burial. He then discovers that she had kept '[a] large album which contained photographs documenting ...almost the whole of Paul Bereyter's life, with notes penned in his own hand.'[14] The overt source of Paul's dislocation emerges in the discovery that he was one quarter Jewish on his father's side, a factor that disqualified him from teaching under the Nuremberg laws. But, despite or perhaps even because of this, he returned to his home country, to Berlin no less, into the lion's den, at the outbreak of the war, in which he could serve even with his racial disability, and resumed his teaching after the war. But he was always consumed by 'a loneliness within',[15] a sense that was presumably to deprive him of

12. Ibid. pp. 16-17.
13. Ibid. p.23.
14. Ibid. p.45.
15. Ibid. p.44.

the will to continue to live. The third section deals with a great uncle of the narrator, Ambros Adelwarth. The narrator had only met him once, but again his curiosity was aroused by photographs.[16] The narrator's Aunt Fini recalls this fascinating character's accounts of the past, when he is visiting the USA. Ambros had fallen into a deep depression, and, of his own free will, had entered a psychiatric sanatorium. This section concludes with a reading of his journal, with which he had been presented by the aunt, from a much earlier period, the year 1913. What he chooses to highlight from that record is the note about memory, that it is 'a kind of dumbness', and that '[i]t makes one's head heavy and giddy.'[17] But the book is all about memory, and it does indeed have that effect. The fourth and final subject of this series of reconstructions and enquiries is the single minded artist Max Ferber, for the purposes of which the narrator takes us back to the time he spent in Manchester, which, for him was a place of fascination and strangeness. Not much is known originally of this Max Ferber, who had erased all memories of a past before he arrived in England at the age of fifteen in 1939. But the narrator catches up with the painter some 25 years later, after he had by chance seen a work of his at the Tate Gallery; Ferber is now an artist much in demand. The return to Manchester in pursuit of his old friend is as bleak as the original contact. But now he receives a memoir from Max penned by his mother many generations ago. The next stage is for the narrator to visit Kissingen, site of the family memoir, and to seek out the Jewish cemetery, where that Jewish community came to an end. The principal feature that the narrator notes in the Germany around him was '[t]he mental impoverishment and lack of memory that marked the Germans.'[18] Unable to bear this any longer, he returns to England, and thus to his own attempt at a memorial.

But the adoption of an ultimate adherence to authenticity can serve very different purposes. Binjamin Wilkomirski's recent work,

---

16. Ibid. p.71.
17. Ibid. p.145.
18. Ibid. p.225.

Fragments,[19] is a long delayed response to the events described in the text, coming fifty years or so after the subject matter contained therein. The title, and its uncertain genre, indicate the apparently impenetrable nature of the material, the difficulty of its absorption and the near impossiblity of its communication. The author attempts to convey his own experiences, those of a child sent to Majdanek to be exterminated, who miraculously and painfully survived, just about, in body. This was against all the odds and against, too, the intentions of the Nazi regime, making such survival not only improbable but also illogical. As the material had not been properly assimilated and absorbed into the author's conscious mind, it could only be brought to the surface very partially, very gradually, and in small pieces, "shards" (as he has it), or "fragments" (hence, the title). But the effort was supremely important for him, and so all means available are conjured up to raise obscured memories into focus. This is a story, but the author's own, a memoir.

Even language constitutes a difficulty. Yiddish is the author's mother tongue, but that was cut off early by the intervention of his camp experience, when he was sent to Majdanek. That language was replaced by what he calls the 'Babel-babble' of the camps, a confused concatenation of tongues, with an admixture of the primary Yiddish. The author's later languages, the adult tongues which superceded his first experience of speech, are not regarded as integrally his own, but rather acquire imitations of foreign voices. More primary then than language indicators for the recovery of this dreadful but transcendent and dominant phase is the instrument of vision. It is the recording eye that can be imprinted on the memory, his own inner "camera", a metaphorical camera, acting in similar ways to the actual cameras of Matalon and Sebald. This is how he builds up this heavily overladen past: 'My early childhood memories are planted, first and foremost, in exact snapshots of my photographic memory and in the feelings imprinted in them, and the physical sensations.'[20] Memory, the recall of the eye, and the impression

---

19. Binjamin Wilkomirski. *Fragments: Memories of a Childhood, 1939-1948.* Translated from the German. Picador. London, 1996. (Original German, 1995). For further analysis of this text, see cap. 9.
20. Ibid. p.4.

created by these, become the organising principle, rather than any other sort of externally imposed logic or chronological sequence. He enters the child's world, because that is the world that has to be recalled. So, in order to achieve the recovery of that world, he has to become a child once more, thus abandoning adult postures, which were a later accretion: 'If I'm going to write about it, I have to give up on the ordering logic of grown-ups; it would only distort what happened.'[21] The object of all this effort is '...to try to use words to draw as exactly as possible what happened, what I saw, exactly the way my child's memory has held on to it; with no benefit of perspective or vantage point.'[22] He wants to reproduce the clear pictures that surface: 'Just pictures, no thoughts attached:'[23]

We must add a rider to this ambition. The pictures are not, to be frank, unaccompanied. There is no doubt that the stark picture itself, without context or clarification for the reader, would hardly make sense. The author does offer at least a minimum of commentary, or, sometimes, some necessary words that allow the reader in on the basis of his own historical orientation. There is then some intervention of an adult observer, looking over the shoulder of the child. But he does hold this to a minimum, attempting to recover the horror, and specifically, the sense of betrayal on the part of the child at the hand of the sadistic adult. He was taken to what he thought was an orphanage, and found himself in a concentration camp. The names for these types of institution were lacking to the child, but the experience can now be conveyed. The child portrayed here gradually loses the childlike mental features. He even loses the capacity to feel: 'There are no feelings left.../I'm just an eye, taking in what it sees, giving nothing back.'[24] The words used are clearly adult words, as are the formulated sentiments. But the feeling behind them can be recaptured. And the feeling that he wants to communicate is of the end of feeling, for that matter, of the end of the world as we have known it: 'I just feel that this is a place where everything ends, not just the embankment and the rails. This is where the world stops

---

21. Ibid.
22. Ibid. pp.4,5.
23. Ibid.
24. Ibid. p.87.

being the world.'[25] It is at such points that the flashbacks are crisscrossed with flashforwards. Later, in Switzerland, where the author was first taken and where he still lives, he looks back on himself with horror at his own apparent lack of feeling, treading over the heads of nursing babies to save himself. The self disgust had reached such proportions that not only had he virtually forgotten his own name, but that he even came to forget that he actually possessed a name. In Switzerland too, he still retained the marks of his background, long after the circumstances of that terror had disappeared. But the child, now presumably becoming a young adult, does not easily grasp the nature of such boundaries, and still sees things in their original terms. That after all was the formative period. Adults, these others, are still the enemies. "Liberation", an adult term, never occurred. The sub-title of the book gives the cut-off point for the subject as 1948, rather than 1945. He has no clear recollection of 1945 as a turning point, but only as a phase when peculiar things started to happen, and when he continued to expect the inevitable calamities. He can never trust anyone. For him, the SS man has invaded the person of the Swiss hero, William Tell, and the child with the apple on his head will be murdered, an act to precede the consumption of the apple by the adult. He is constantly told to forget. But he can never forget, and he rather needs to verify his own experience continually in order to check it against the accounts of others. For this reason, he can only find genuine communication with those whose experiences match his own. The act of writing here, the setting down of his story to the best of his ability and as truthfully as he can, is a necessary act of purgation, a sort of belated self-discovery.

---

25. Ibid. p.94.

The New Israeli Novel

One of the typical new novels in Israel is constituted of an exercise in memorialisation. In Judith Katzir's *Lematis yesh et hashemesh babeten* (Matisse has the Sun in his Belly),[26] a love story is not only recorded long after the event, but searched out, fixed in the memory, memorialised. Rather than integrated into the life of the principal character, the lovely Rivi, twenty-one years old at the time of the affair, the story is elevated as the high point and guiding light of her life. Rivi falls in love with a much older man, Yigal, her mentor, a lecturer in Mathematics at the Haifa Technion. It is Yigal who is specifically marked out by a search for place, he whose original home was not Israel, but somewhere in Central Europe. Rivi can get her habit of yearning from him, as she can learn so many other things too. And this makes "yearning" the central theme of the novel, the looking back to a time or place that was. Rivi then goes with Yigal to Europe, and becomes his lover. They go to Italy and to Paris, and the photos that they take there become the sign and monument of the formative phase of her life: 'And she was already longing for this house that she was leaving behind her, not that she might be coming back here in a week or two's time, but as though she had lost it forever, as she would long for it following the passage of many years.'[27] Here, the expected mark in memory becomes a fact of life, and establishes her very being. In the "Italian" chapter, there is a flash forward, and we read: 'Often would she pore over their photographs - what else have I got left apart from them'[28], she asks herself. The problem is that experience in its actuality is so short-lived. Even whilst the affair is taking place, the person undergoing it is aware of its transience, and feels the need to perpetuate its sense and texture. This has become the function of the photograph. But this is reflected in the title of the novel as well, where the title phrase, i.e. that Matisse has the sun in his belly (as reportedly uttered by Picasso), becomes a motto for the book, and becomes the model for

---

26. Judith Katzir, *Lematis yesh et hashemesh babeten*. Hakkibutz hameuhad. Tel Aviv, 1996.
27 Ibid. p.34.
28. Ibid. p.43.

her supreme experience. It is not only Rivi, however, who draws out the past here. She manages to extract memories from her partner, memories that he has hitherto buried deep inside himself. Time is then not equally spread in its significance, and this short time span, the snatched holiday in Europe, becomes the hinge of the central figure, and so of the book as a whole. The uneven quality of time is a recurrent theme in modernist writing. Of course, moments of significance have always been afforded a greater degree of focus; events are not treated equally, then to receive an equivalent amount of space deriving from their proportional extent. But now, there is heightened awareness of the erratic impression made separately by various time spans, as captured by memory and recall. These "fragments" are an extreme exemplification of such recognition.

Rivi looks both backwards and forwards; her memorialisation is the recollection of the past and also protection against the vicissitudes of the future. She can proceed to a new life henceforth, following the passing away of her mother and the end of her affair with Yigal. The flashes forward shadow the future,[29] with the significance of the pictures as evidence to imprint memory for a later period.[30] Her passion is unique, not to be repeated, so it must be recoverable as a thing that was.[31] In terms of narrative perspective, the voices alternate as between the first person, when the emotion is not contained, and the detached third person. All the trips that they have made together, (these are the high points of their passionate union, as they were then together, isolated, separate from others, intensively and extensively together). The Egypt, which she also can recall as being the country associated with her grandfather, is appropriately mummified, embalmed in her recollection. This all becomes a monument for the future.

Her attempts at memorialisation of her lover constitute a considerable part of the novel, pictures and all.[32] She is informed by the haunting figure of the fortune teller in Tel Aviv that something of this necessarily doomed affair will always remain. The past then,

---

29. Ibid.
30. Ibid. p.48.
31. Ibid. p.77.
32. Ibid. p.162.

however it is sealed up, confined, and cast away, will always be with her. Yigal too appreciates this, and what he values in her is precisely her capacity to preserve this kernel, and to make something of it in written form:'"It is in this that your power lies, in inscribing the meteorological map of your stormy soul."'.[33] This is said in the wake of their separation. What is preserved as a residue is precisely the book. So the novel here, in front of the reader, is the replay of what is recorded in that original document.

In another new Israeli novel, Eleanora Lev's *Haboqer harishon began eden* (First Morning in Paradise),[34] takes the form of a sort of a long memoir, built up around the female narrator and her married lover. There is a detailed dissection of her own feelings, and a meditation on her loss of youth and attractiveness. She leaves home for an apartment, so as to acquire the necessary freedom of manoeuvre. She mourns the loss of her lover, Saul, as well as the loss that he represents to Hebrew drama, to which he had contributed so much as one of Israel's leading playwrights. And there is too the wife's loss, contrasted with the narrator's own different sort of loss.[35] The chaos of Tel Aviv, as described here[36] (pp. 131-4), acts as an objective correlative to her own feelings, as does her description of the impoverishment of immigrant life. The inevitable happens, and she waits , as she says 'like a piece of meat' for an abortion. She is an 'eshet tselalim' (shadow wife), or a 'gevavah urbanit shelahar yeush' (urban heap in the wake of despair,[37] in regard to Tel Aviv). We have the relationship between the pictorial representation and the verbal; where the sometimes more accurate and penetrating equivalent of words is a photograph, although this latter is supplemented by the words. The photograph is the attempt to grasp the moment, and imprint it on the memory;[38] Ira Bernowitz, her friend and advisor, presses in one direction, arguing strongly that an abortion is an

33. Ibid. p.187.
34. Eleanora Lev, *Haboqer harishon began eden*. (First Morning in Paradise). Tel Aviv, 1996.
35. Ibid. p.284.
36. Ibid. pp.131-134.
37. Ibid. p.303.
38. Ibid. p.260.

absolute necessity, whilst her own instincts move her the other way. She has become convinced that she needs the life of the child to supplement her uncertain vitality. The text is addressed to the new life, the potential and then the actual child, from conception leading up to birth. At the end, she is visited by the memory of a picture of Eve, set down in Eden (hence the title). She (the narrator) even comes to terms with the basic human fact of male domination, because, if she could had not been able to; 'Then, in that event, she would never bear a child: it was this hunger that was decisive.' (these are the closing words of the novel – 'haraav hazeh hu shehikhria et hakaf').

Shifra Horn, in her novel *Arba imahot* (Four Mothers),[39] adopts a very complex and subtle narrative approach. The first person narrator is born in the Summer of 1948, in Jerusalem. The mother of the narrator is Geulah, the father is "unknown". Amal, the narrator, grows up in an atmosphere where her mother is hostile to boys. She herself marries Yaakov, who leaves her when the son is born. This Yaakov believes in his multiple genetic role, as strongest male, and so when that particular function is fulfilled, he can leave and search for another female.

The four successive mothers raise children by themselves. Amal's own son breaks the pattern of the exclusively female line. The first recorded member of this line, Mazal, flourished a hundred years earlier, bore Sara (the beauty and central figure of the novel), and was then divorced, aged sixteen, for not providing satisfaction to her husband. Sara had an ongoing affair with the British Edward, a well known photographer, whose brilliant daughter was Pnina-Mazal. Pnina-Mazal married David, who was killed. Her daughter, Geulah, grew up wild, and remained, in later life too, exclusively attached to the Arab child with whom she is reared. In the Israeli context, it was understandable that she then turned into a revolutionary. But she was then raped, and her baby, called Amal (the name functions well as a common name both in Hebrew and in Arabic) is our narrator here. She wants to discover her origins, and produces an oral transmission from a member of a Communist cell that she joins, by means of a

---

39. Shifra Horn, *Arba imahot.* (Four Mothers.) Maariv. Tel Aviv, 1996.

tape recorder.[40] Sara, the great grandmother, feels that she can die when new baby boy is born. This is the end of the saga of the **mothers**. The son, unnamed still with the conclusion of the novel, brings this exclusively matrilineal tradition to an end. Amal's son marks both the novel's termination and the end of this deviant line.

The view of the place of the woman here is unexpected. We are accustomed to seeing Feminism as a modern phenomenon, with the stress that it places on, either the equality of the sexes or, going beyond that, the primacy of the female. But here, the further that we go back in time, the greater is the degree of female domination, and it is only as we approach our own time that the male seems to come into his own. Now, arriving at the contemporary scene, i.e. the period of the composition of the novel, the balance of the genders is restored.

Irit Linur is one of the new brand of demotic female Israeli novelists, a writer conveying the material in the common language of current Israeli speech. Her first novel, *Shirat hasirenah* (The Siren's Song)[41] is written in a local argot, related in the first person as though a diary, straight from the sleeve. The narrator has a feeling that she is aging (the narrator is 32 years old), a common enough obsession in life as in literature. She works as a senior administrator, responsible for budgets, in an Advertising Agency. The novel presents an unfiltered ego, through the medium of idiomatic language, and articulates uninhibited thought. She, the narrator, offers a deflated view of herself, witty, self-effacing, fully admitting to the need for love, and thus to her own limitations.

The diary genre offers a medium of memorialisation. It records directly and confidentially. It does not have to pass through the sieve of public acceptability, or stand before the court of public opinion. It is, by definition, addressed to oneself. It can remain unembarrassed and unencumbered by structural or conventional considerations. The introduction of the diary form (or quasi diary form) into the novel can offer a glimpse of narrative intimacy not normally granted to the

---

40. Ibid. p.262.
41. Irit Linur. *Shirat hasirenah*. (The Siren Song). Zmora-Bitan. Tel Aviv, 1991.

reader, and thus extend the imaginative and expressive borders of the genre.

The question is often raised as to whether there is a distinctly feminine fictional voice in Israeli literature. But the sheer quantity of this production, amounting to predominance, testifies to the growing strength and confidence of the Israeli woman writer. But we may still pose the question of whether there is a qualitative difference from the male voice.

From what we have seen here, the expression of this tendency is characteristically Israeli in language, character and in tone. But it is non-ideological, except to assert the strength of the needs of the woman, the narrator or the prime mover in the story. There has been a shift of focus. The shift is from the consideration of such weighty themes as, for example, the Jew as Israeli, the place of Israel in the world, or the place of the fighting soldier. This does not mean that the woman does not play a central role in fiction by male writers. The feminine figure is certainly important in, for example, the work of the well known male novelist, Amos Oz. But there, she is an object of interest, the representation of the unpredictable and the mysterious, very much the "other". In the work discussed here, the point of view adopted is that of the woman, taken on as natural, central, the assumed given. Desire, love, emotional fulfilment, the needs of woman, lover, mother are primary and all encompassing. Interpersonal relationships, rather than symbolic function or national allegory, come up for critical inspection. Domestic themes stand out here; sex, love, growing up, growing old, the nature of changing affections, death and memory. These are what invest the narrator and the fiction with such zest as they possess and evince.

And in France

Patrick Modiano (b. Paris, 1945, mother – Flemish, father – a Sefardi Jew) is a contemporary French writer. An early work of his is entitled *La Place de l'Etoile,*[42] which can stand for various things. The "place" of the title name can imply - square, badge or heart. The name of the "hero", Schlemilovitch, indicates his own, status, shlemiel (the ne'er do well), but also ensures that this particular Jew can don a variety of guises; martyr, king, clown, and, also, avenger. He always remains a foreigner, because he bears that dislocated experience within. The novel is written in the first person. The main character, our Schlemilovitch, abandons his Venezuelan background, is a foreigner in France, and is known widely as a Jew: 'Aux journalistes qui me questionnaient devant le *Carlton,* le *Normandy* ou le *Miramar,* je proclamais inlassablement ma juiverie,' he says (To the jounalists who question me in front of the Carlton, the Normandy or the Miramar, I proclaim my Jewishness indefatiguably, p.14). He wants to be a great, French Jewish writer. But now: 'Le juif était une marchandise prisée, on nous respectait trop. Je pouvais entrer à Saint-Cyr et devenir le maréchal Sclemilovitch: l'affaire Dreyfus ne recommencera pas.' (The Jew is acceptable merchandise, everyone respects us too much. I can go into Saint-Cyr and become Marshall Schlemilovitch: the Dreyfus Afffair won't come back again.)'[43] In the later, prize-winning novel too, the *Rue des Boutiques Obscures*[44], the main character, deprived of identity, sets out, as a detective (his profession, appropriately enough), in search of his past, his existence, and, therefore, his identity. Guy Roland: 'sur la piste de mon passé.' (on the track of my past).[45] Once more, the narrative is presented in the first person, although we have a heavily disguised narrator. The novel opens with the words: 'Je ne sais rien. Rien qu'une silhouette claire, ce soir là, à la terrasse d'un café.' (I know nothing. There was nothing but a distinct silhouette on that evening, on the café

---

42. Patrick Modiano. *La Place de l'Etoile*. Gallimard. Paris, 1968.
43. Ibid. p.38.
44. Patrick Modiano. *Rue des Boutiques Obscures*. Gallimard. Paris, 1978.
45. Ibid. p.14.

terrace.)[46] The sense of a dislocated Jew, seeking a location is reminiscent of Romain Gary, the great French novelist of an earlier generation, born in Vilnius, in his novel, *La Danse de Genghis Cohn*,[47] where the executed Jew, Moishe, also known as Genghis Cohn (although "murdered" by the Nazis) cannot die, and so, after the war, invades the body of the Nazi officer, Schatz. In this novel, the torment and the unresolved tensions are exemplified in a metaphor become grotesque reality. Present day Germany, in this view, has not absorbed (that is to say, not totally consumed, swallowed) the events of previous years. Rather than state this in banal and transparent language, the author vividly encapsulates this notion through the penetration of the clownish Moishe into the physical body of the Nazi. But the form of presentation seems to tease the reader, and leave him in some doubt as to whether what is offered is a memoir, a diary, or a fiction. These are the narrative options, where the lines of demarcation merge into each other.

We normally associate a diary with uncensored recording of feeling, where there is no need for disguise, and so where the truth is more likely to emerge. The author after all does not have to feel that there is a reader looking over his shoulder, and so he might be at liberty to offer an unvarnished version of the narrative that he offers. A novel, on the other hand, as the term "fiction" suggests, can be the product of the imagination, in the traditional sense of invented material. We certainly would not rebuke the author of fiction for lying about the factual material conveyed. A memoir, though, does make a claim to veracity, and the reader might expect literal truth in its pages. However, unlike a diary, it is not a private work; it is presented to the public. What seems to be happening in recent work is that the boundaries traditionally erected are collapsing in the search for new forms of presentation.

It might be thought that the discussion so far has revolved around empty questions of technique rather than content, that we have been dealing with the "how" rather than with the "what". However, the variety of technical resources brought to bear on the

46. Ibid. p.11.
47. Romain Gary. *La Danse de Genghis Cohn*. Gallimard. Paris, 1968.

material itself predicates new needs, as well as a dissatisfaction with what is already in place. The writer has to invoke new and multiple ways of achieving the desired effects. But there is naturally a wide range of disparate concerns represented in the literature. Some of it aspires to reveal the turmoil of the individual, and the need to impress the significance of external events on personal development. In the case of other types of writing, personal concerns may play no smaller part, but the implications may have public and political reverberations. Both are significant in equal measure, and the writer makes the effort to seek out the means adequate for their expression.

Turns of the Novel

The evidence of current writing does not square with the notion of the death of the novel. The novel is taking on new forms, and presents the narrative in many guises. What is distinctive about the novel as a genre is its cultivation of a cognate relationship of the novel form to the contemporary setting. That is to say that the novel is adjacent to the recognisable life as lived by common humanity. It comments on it, whilst preserving the necessary distance in order to sharpen the objective (the view from the outside) perception of character and its development. The flexibility of language, shift of scene, deployment of paradoxical devices, options of time and space, and the involvement of the reader, can shift the perspective, deepen understanding, and open the mind to differences of approach. This takes us back to the original discussion and to the question of generic distinctions within literature. The fact is accompanied by the commentary, explicit or implicit. There can be no statement without a narrator, the one who frames the statement. An event has its meaning, otherwise we would not record it in human terms for human consumption and understanding.

This is made manifest in our modern fiction, where additional materials are brought to bear on the text. These do not veil the voice of the narrator, but they do provide supplementary sources of bombardment that are designed to concretise the narrative. Whether this may deepen the experience of the reader or not, may be an open question. On that issue the reader will no doubt arrive at an independent judgement. But, as is the case with all such innovation, possibilities like these can certainly broaden the range of available narrative technique. It is this range which is being explored and exploited in current fiction.

VIII

MOURNING THE PAST IN CURRENT ISRAELI FICTION

Looking Back

Although Israel is very young as an independent State, it still sees itself as in possession of a long history, divided conceptually into periods and phases. The iconography and mythology in official and semi-official historiography tend to confirm this view. There are the precursors of Zionism, then there is pre-Settlement Zionism, accompanied by the founding fathers of the first and early settlements. Following this, there is the phase of the "State on the Way", also known as Mandatory Palestine, succeeded by the establishment of the State of Israel itself. This is viewed officially in hallowed distance. The State was then built up and compounded by later waves of immigration from the Middle East, North Africa, to some extent from the West, from the Soviet Union, from Ethiopia and from many other lands. This process constantly resounded to the echoes of the continuous war(s) with the Arab world and, on the local front, with the indigenous Arab/Palestinian population. These factors have constituted the ongoing prelude and backdrop to contemporary Israel, a subject in itself.

In literature too, and especially in fiction, Israeli writers, through the narrative voices in their work, create a picture of a current society, looking back to a more impressive past. However recent this past may be in literal terms, it sometimes seems light years away in ethos and atmosphere. A contrast is drawn between this "once upon a time" world" and the grey, even sordid, reality of the present. Specifically, it is felt that there had once existed genuine idealism and an epoch, when the people of the Land, even through the stark fact of being settlers, had once been heroes. The literature of the Israeli nation bears eloquent testimony to such a perception.

This tendency has been articulated for some decades now in the early work of such novelists as Benjamin Tammuz (1919-1989) and Yehoshua Knaz (1937-), in the two novels (the second published posthumously and incomplete) of Yaakov Shabtai (1934-1981), in novels by Nathan Shaham (1925-), in the lyrical fiction of Shulamith Hareven, and also in the ongoing work of Aharon Megged (1920-) and Meir Shalev (1948-). Sometimes, the sentiment is conveyed satitrically, sometimes ironically, but, very often too, with genuine nostalgia.[1]

Nathan Shaham has dwelt, in his extensive and ongoing fiction, on the sense of history, and his subject has been – the individual caught up in the swell of forces beyond his control. His novel, *Lev tel-aviv* (The Heart of Tel-Aviv),[2] is conveyed in the third person, by a retired Foreign Office official, recalled to service for a project in Tunisia. The narrator is concerned both with the state of the nation and the condition of his family, in the effort of the central character to unravel and reconstruct the past. He recalls his contact with a reality that had been veiled in abstractions. The "saving remnant" of modern Jewish mythology was seen as a series of suffering individuals with pathetic stories to tell.[3] Ideology is constantly forced into confrontation with the messier features of actuality. Modern Jewish and Israeli history are composed of an amalgam of ideologies and separate stories. This is Shaham's theme in his fictional portraits of the past and present, as well as of the past in the present. This is what makes him such a political writer. His fictional characters are drawn in different, sometimes opposite directions, embracing abstract ideologies, and then living them out. The principal theoretical doctrines with which his characters engage are Socialism and

1. For a brief account of this theme, see Leon I. Yudkin, *Beyond Sequence.* Symposium Press. London, 1992, pp. 29-44.
2. Nathan Shaham, *Lev tel-aviv*. Am Oved. Tel-Aviv, 1996.
3. Ibid. p.84.

Zionism, the former often of the Soviet mould. Thus, these people are concerned with the regeneration and reform of the human race on the one hand, and/or with the revolution and transformation of the Jewish nation on the other.

In "The Heart of Tel-Aviv", the principal character, Avner, who has retrained as a lawyer, implicitly an archetype of selfish and cynical opportunism, has himself gone through such processes. That he was very susceptible to ideological modification, is indicated by the ease with which, initially, as a youngster, he fell, fascinated, into the clutches of the extremist, Jewish nationalist movement, the *Irgun,* and then, just as suddenly, took his place in the pioneering, kibbutz orientated mainstream, the ideological opponent of the *Irgun.* All this is recounted in his review of past life. More importantly though, his mental and emotional being becomes enmeshed in his external biography, his relationship with women and his parents. All these come to the service of the search for the core of his own identity. Thus, large parts of the novel become an exposition and detailed breakdown of motive, event and analysis, *apologia* and *récherche.* From this, the reader bears witness to the internal struggles, doubts compromises and transformations of such a politically aware Israeli. Ideology and life become biography or disguised autobiography. The author presents a portrait of a character type, where the life style and affiliations echo character. The basis presented for his selection of a new loyalty is his cautious and qualified sense of balance, his '[r]ecognition that nothing was either completely right or completely wrong' and 'that suited his sceptical nature.'[4] So the transition to a very different sort of ideological association, with a very different sort of policy, was not effected so much on the basis of an assessment of the rights and wrongs of the case, but rather stemmed from his own inherent character traits. But, of course, it is only with the maturity of years and in the growing distance from the events described, that such a judgment may be passed. This is one of the features that distinguishes this kind of retrospective reflection from a text composed in the white heat of possessive passion.

---

4. Ibid. p.138.

The novel, which relates to various phases of the life of the main character, goes from flashback to flash forward, focusing on the principal issue of his relationship to his father, the painter. For these purposes, the latter's artistic heritage is made the focus. We see the way fortunes and fashions change, how the father, beyond the grave, grows in dimension and in reputation, and how the son devotes himself to creating a suitable memorial for the parent, with some of the proceeds from sales of his paintings. The reader may wonder what sort of person is this Avner, who can shift so easily ideologically and spiritually. He seems so different from his friend Elkanah, that his wife, Michal, asks how Elkanah could have been close to one who was evidently '[w]ithout a crystallised outlook and principles.'[5] But is Avner really lacking such a frame? Or, is it not rather that a growing individual is also one who changes? Perhaps, political outlook and ideology can adjust their contours to match changing circumstances and character. It seems that the best parts of the novel, those truest and most authentic, are those which tell of the hero's emotional condition. We can see this in the love scene with Marianne[6], where the text flows most smoothly, without the recourse to explicit and unwieldy exposition that clogs up so much of a Shaham text. It is in such parts that the characters attempt to recapture their childhood love. The political meeting turns into an emotional outpouring. Avner is at this stage working for the Israeli Foreign Office, and he is assigned to find out more about the revolutionary organisations with which Marianne has been associated. She, as a Communist activist, had gone off to the Soviet Union, and then been imprisoned in Siberia, whilst still retaining her initial faith.

The novel, paricularly through Avner's lens, raises the notion of the mythologising of the past. Israel's brief history has become the foundation of this mythology, spiritual and theoretical. But, is the notion of myth not rather a comfortable name for "lies"? The episode of the murder of Bella Zeidman, who may have been his lover, as she had gone through numerous liaisons, is assumed to have been the

5. Ibid. p.192.
6. Ibid. pp.238-241.

responsibility of the Revisionist groups. They had worked, in their different and various ways, for the expulsion of the British and the establishment of the Jewish State. Avner had been associated with these groups, until he made his sideways move into the respectable territory of the *Haganah* and the *Palmach*. Now, many years on, he is consulted by a young historian for his views on that event. Avner thus researches the past and its place in the present. One of his sons by his first wife, Ram, a highly respected historian of the ancient world, sees Israel as a sort of Sparta, whereas he himself would be more at ease in Athens. What is Avner's position in all this? Is his framework ensured and recognised? Many perspectives have to be taken into account in order to arrive at any overall assessment. There is the view of the women, the assumed perspective of Enosh, victim of the Yom Kippur war, the extreme Nationalist view of his old associate, Dror, who played such a substantial part in shaping his youth, and who certainly had been involved in Bella's death. The past still inhabits the present, and leaves its imprint on all phases of current experience. The novel ends, when the project to collect the father's paintings, is to come to fruition with the support of an old and rediscovered acquaintance. This will take the form of a site that will not only house the paintings, but is also to be a music centre and literary venue. Avner challenges the view expressed that: 'Only the person whose future is ending starts to take an interest in the past.'[7] with an assertion of the essential continuity that must be sought. This is what the project should seek to serve. This is presumably also Avner's own hard won view of life's function, and the means that he has discovered to unite the attitudes and lives of his father, his sons, and of his own wavering loyalties.

---

7. Ibid. p.378.

Old Scores of the New Settlement

Much of recent Hebrew fiction has been dealing with the early stages of Hebrew settlement in Palestine, going back to the 1880s, known in Zionist historiography as the first aliyah. It has always been a problem for the modern Hebrew novel that there has been a lack of substantial continuity within one place that could allow the possibility of the traditional family saga. Jewish life has been so refracted and interrupted, subject to external forces and tides. This particularly pertains to the area of the Holy Land, arena of the Israeli drama and locus of the contemporary Hebrew writer. It is indeed not surprising that the Hebrew writer now should cast a fresh eye over what is, by comparative standards, recent history. But, however it appears from the outside, for the Israeli, this is the foundation narrative. Megged, Tammuz and Knaz, amongst others, have treated this phase in great depth. However limited the geographical extent of the territory under consideration and however relatively short the time span of Israel's history, this is modern Israel's source and the basis of the new State. For this reason, it is of fundamental concern.

The specific contribution of Meir Shalev to this genre is the addition of an element of the grotesque. This is combined with an original grasp of the (literally, as well as metaphorically) underground origin of the process of settlement expansion. Shalev's first novel, *Roman rusi* (A Russian Novel),[8] is a saga of a moshav, comprising a retrospective of village life. The narrative plunges the reader straight into the plot and the characters with an immediate surprise and shock, when the calm of the village night is broken by someone's exultant cries that he has been screwing "Lieberson's granddaughter". When the veteran teacher, Yaakov Pines, indignantly charges out to restore order, we have the scene set. Tradition and values are to be reasserted against the undermining intrusions of the dark forces. But it is also a fact that the moment such a line is established, it is immediately challenged. Shalev's novel sets out to offer an ongoing appraisal that charts this story, without sentimental-

---

8. Meir Shalev, *Roman rusi*. Am Oved. Tel-Aviv, 1988. The pagination given here refers to this edition. There is also an English translation, *The Blue Mountain.* Harper Collins. New York, 1991.

ity and with black humour. Appropriately, the first thing that happens to the respected teacher as he storms out in his righteous search for the culprit, is that he stumbles. What has brought about his fall is the "underground" activity of a mole, creating cavities in the soil for the unsuspecting pedestrian.[9] The anonymous cry is not simply an isolated, let alone innocent, action; it constitutes an incitement to deviation, tempting us to stray from the true path, in order to follow the facile temptations of the flesh. The new codes of behaviour, self-indulgent and lawless, are accompanied by the cynical and mocking laughs of the hyena. This animal, for Pines, assumes the proportions of a sinister symbol. It derives from beyond the wheat fields and the blue mountain, i.e. from beyond the range of the civilisation that has been established so painstakingly. Many had been bitten by the dreadful beast, and they had been duly infected. Some had abandoned the land and moved out to the cities. Others had died or emigrated. Thus, the situation in the village, as perceived by the old didact and pioneer, becomes a metaphor for the condition of the Israeli State. It struggles to hold on to the founding ideology in the face of the new threats. Pines is a type of the old ideologue, representative of the original spirit that moved the immigrants to face a hostile, harsh, but unavoidable environment. There are enemies on all sides; parasites, messianists and communists. They can only be resisted with the full force of the passionate ideals of the founding fathers, whose message, Pines, almost a lone herald, desperately promotes. The parallels between the hyena and the human traitors who have abandoned the project, are brought out explicitly.[10] Others in the village though tend rather to the mental and physical decline of the old man. We have the assertion of the ideology and, then almost immediately, its challenge.

We see that the narrative perspective adopted derives from a later epoch, two generations beyond. The first person narrator, Baruch Senhar, is the grandson of Mirkin, another member of the moshav, where the story is set. He is a contemporary of Pines. At the opening of the narrative, Baruch is fifteen years old, and had grown

9. Ibid. p.6.
10. Ibid. p.7.

up within the confines of the agricultural, Zionist atmosphere, reared by his grandfather. The child had been orphaned at the age of two, when his parents had been murdered by Arab marauders. The grandfather had eagerly assumed the parental role, and reared the grandson to fulfill his own needs. We only gradually discover all the details pertaining to the familial background. But the source of discovery and the narrative focus are the grandfather and grandson. The former is from the old world and a member of the second aliyah, a wave of Zionist immigration even more ideologically orientated than the first, pioneering, socialist, and dourly nationalist. The latter was born and bred as a Hebrew farmer in what had been the land of dreams and aspirations, but had become now a hard, wild territory, suitable for the reconstituted Jew. This narrative device, skipping over the generation of the absent, because murdered parents, sets the new generation alongside, not that of its natural and expected preceding cadre, but alongside the one previous. That had been the generation when the pioneering, Zionist ideology was still dominant, before the rot set in. This positioning grants the narrator a privileged place both within the narrative frame itself, and on its fringes, as an observer from beyond. Thus the reader can partake simultaneously of "then" and "now". Baruch has also gained the reputation of one who is always listening in, attendant on the affairs of others, and thus can be regarded as a constant if not reliable witness. Pines sees it as a sign of his personal failure that the younger generation/s should behave in such a manner as to discredit and undermine his own tutelage. "'They (i.e. the parents) will come and blame me'", he laments,[11] comparing himself to a farmer, and his young charges to delicate plants, which he himself had failed in the inadequate discharge of his responsibilities.

The young narrator, Baruch, differs from so many other first person narrators, in that he does not merely reflect the expected authorial stance. He is neither a writer nor an intellectual of any kind, but rather a very solid type, notable for his great strength and physical prowess. He is known to be rather stupid. Meshulam Zirkin, whom the narrator naturally hated, used to pat him on the shoulder,

---

11. Ibid. p.12.

and say of him: "Why so little intelligence and so much flesh?"[12] And we will see that later too, he cannot cope with the technicalities of modern living, with cheques and foreign languages. That is why he has to engage an assistant, the all knowing, variously competent, Busquila, a new immigrant from Morocco, to handle all his affairs. But although Baruch is rather gross and primitive, again unlike most fictional narrators, who customarily bear a remarkable resemblance to their authors, his intelligence allows him to make a shrewd assessment of the needs and aspirations of the village community. And this assessment culminates in the conclusion that this population will only become a true community in historical terms when it possesses its own cemetery. The cemetery too becomes a highly prized object of desire, and thus it is seen to be a mark of special recognition and favour to be buried there. In recognition of this, burial is strictly restricted to those who came to the Land in the second wave, this so-called second aliyah, which granted the settlement its pioneering base within that period, 1904-1909. Special prestige attaches to this select group, and even those who remained only briefly in the Land before going off to make their subsequent fortunes in America, are willing to pay huge sums for the privilege of burial in this earth. Thus, the house of death becomes the source of life for Baruch, as the graves become the foundation of the authentic community. This is the paradox that lies at the heart of the novel.

Baruch understands the motor force of the community, what makes it tick, and he can turn that understanding to his own benefit. We see him as a youngster and in his maturity, as the novel takes us through the generations. The work is written on two time scales, set, on the one hand, in his early youth, and then, in his maturity. It is a "Russian novel", as its origin derives from the Russian characters, and it is a "Russian romance",[13] telling the stories of these founders, their descendants and their relationships. The village, and particularly the cemetery, becomes a tourist centre, and visitors stream there in their thousands to see the relics of the old life. Baruch, who relays

---

12. Ibid. p.21.
13. The Hebrew title of the novel, "Roman rusi", is ambiguous, meaning either "Russian novel" or "Russian romance", as the Hebrew word, "roman", deriving of course from European languages, means both things, and thus alludes to both.

the narrative, is the auditor of so many stories passed on by his grandfather, tales of times long ago. He keeps hearing about his family too, although his deeper curiosity in regard to his immediate forbears is never truly satisfied. There is a deep wound at the heart of the grandfather, and he bears a resentment that is only satisfied by the grandson's success through the soil. This constitutes revenge, as it is now his line which makes the decisions of life and death, and thus holds the vital cards. Everyone wants finally to be integrated into the land. But they can only achieve that at the whim of the slightly backward Baruch, at great expense, and then only in death. This is another expression of "living on the dead", as the third generation feeds off the stock of the grandfather, Mirkin, next to whom everyone seeks to be buried.[14] They, of that generation of the "founding fathers", had accumulated very little in their own lifetimes, whereas their contemporaries elsewhere had so much. But, in death, those who had drifted so far away seem to aspire above all to return. The new, young life too looks back to this original stock, as to the only source available, from which it sprung. Whether there is genuine or only illusory value in this source we, as readers and observers have to make our own judgments. Baruch can make his on the basis of the stories that he hears and the incidents that he recounts, twin material that he transmits onwards, to the reader. Pines, who is the filter for much of the narrative, points out that in fact there have been two separate settlements established: '[t]he village and the cemetery, and both of them will continue to grow.'[15] This is another way of saying that personal death, as held within the space by the residue of the body, is the only possible guarantor of life in the future. The veteran teacher acts as a witness and contemporary chronicler of the ideational decrepitude of the village.

The downside is that the life that is passed on is by no means a spiritual heir to those founders. The second generation of settlers very quickly displays symptoms of decay and corruption. They are known as the "gang";[16] they rob, they vandalise, and generally make life a misery for their elders and peers. Nature too takes its course,

---

14. *Roman rusi*, p.40.
15. Ibid. p.73.
16. Ibid. p.98.

and the hyena constantly mocks our cast of characters, providing a baleful commentary to the proceedings. The corruption of the natural world indeed serves as metaphor for the universal scene, specifically as it is manifested in the village, which, in its turn, can stand for the Israeli and the pre-Israeli community. The narrator's father, Benjamin, has carried a civilisation with him from Germany, hardly adjusting to the harsh and different circumstances of Palestine. But he is quickly out of the picture, and our guardian of the grave, Baruch, has his contact in the main with two generations back, with the original spring of the Zionist revolution. This had been not only a revolution, but a cultural, geographical, historical and spiritual rupture, which our narrative must communicate.

Many times the narrator steps out of the story in order to comment on his purposes, albeit indirectly. We learn about him that he is isolated within a community, and that this had blurred the initially clear outline of his grandfather's image, which his purpose was to convey.[17] For the lack of a consistent and true conception he has to rely more on single shafts of memory. For example, his grandfather had saved his life by killing off a prowling hyena when the child was only three years old. This heroic incident had been reported in the Hebrew press, and thus becomes a verifiable source for the reader. Yaakov Mirkin then is a hero, not just for the narrator, but for the whole community of settlers, and so enters the mythology of the Movement as one of the great founding fathers. The narrator himself remains always a puzzle to those around him, and they regard him as unfathomable and mysterious.[18] He had always been separated from his peer group, an unfortunate fact which Pines attributes to the possessive and obsessive influence of his grandfather, which the old man refused relinquish. But now, at the age of thirty-eight, at the time of presenting this narrative, he still regards himself, once and for all, in perpetuity, as the pupil of Pines and the child of the grandfather.[19] Thus the myth is not only sealed and confirmed by its subject and presenter, but by its manner of telling and the voice. The voice, as it is presumably rendered in the novel, is the voice of those who

17. Ibid. p.166.
18. Ibid. p.193.
19. Ibid. p.196.

established the colony and set the tone, a tone albeit filtered by a somewhat limited denizen of the disciples and grandchildren. We are witness not only to the events described, but also to the stature of those conveying the story. So we may also bear witness to the unstated but implied decline in the spiritual power of the newer generation.

And Once there was Peace

Clearly, a central feature of the remembered (or imagined) past is of a peace that once reigned. Within the very fractious, hostile and sometimes hysterical environment, the contemporary eye is bound to search for tranquillity. The constant war experience by Israel has set virtual neighbour against neighbour; suspicion and enmity reign, as fear and aggression stalk the public domain. The slogans reach falsetto pitch, and any sense of nationhood precludes the "other" communities. Specifically, Israel, through its ruling parties and official policy, has become more and more of a "Jewish" State in the exclusivist sense, seeking to remove the ethnicities not belonging to this category, from any part in the collective polity.

Some however look back to a time when this was not the case. Such a time, according to this view, was not so long ago, well within the memory span of the present population. A novel which expresses this mood is Shulamith Hareven's *Le yamim rabim*, (City of Many Days).[20] It is a work of joy and high spirits, recalling a period of less than thirty years prior to the time of composition, when Jerusalem (the subject of the novel) was a genuinely multi-ethnic community, in which flourished, to some extent a degree of mutual appreciation and understanding, or, at least, the aspiration towards this situation. The novel has a long cast list for such a short work. We are first introduced to Don Yitzhak Amirillo, father of Sarah, the main character and principal narrative voice. It is Amirillo who sets the scene and the tone, which is gradually transformed and changes into

---

20. Shulamith Hareven, *Ir yamim rabim*. Am Oved. Tel-Aviv, 1972. It was published in English as *City of Many Days*. Doubleday. New York, 1977.

a sort of elegy. The narrator looks back on a Jerusalem which was once "cordial" (nilbav), and in which the Don was the most cordial of all. He burst with the joy of life, collects children like an oriental Gulliver in Lilliput, and finds it hard to resist women. From time to time, he spawns more children outside marriage, to the great grief of his long suffering spouse, Garcia, who, at the same time, is giving birth to children by him. And so we have a scene; Oriental, Occidental, Jewish, Arab, a combination of old and new settlements, pioneering, secular and traditional. But all is not well, if you dig beneath the surface. Amirillo disappears with the mysterious French "countess", who had come from the Lebanon to organise an exhibition of paintings, that then seemed inexplicably to disappear. He had seemed to be such a pleasant, welcoming and charming man, just as Jerusalem had been such an open, cosmopolitan and pleasant, although albeit provincial, town, under Ottoman and Mandatory rule. But odd things were always going on subterraneously. The wife, Garcia, is left stranded, "anchored" in Jewish legal terminology, thus not free to remarry, and ever more miserable. It seems that she had always been resentful of her husband, despite his apparent charm and universal popularity. But, as far as she was concerned, this ubiquitous affability had not been extended to her, and her situation became untenable.

But this is a story about people who come to Jerusalem from all sorts of different places, and thus form the peculiar composite fabric of the city. It is then a story more about the town, with its changing fortunes and atmosphere, than about specific individuals. Another important element is the German immigration, and we have Dr. Heinz Barzel, familiarly known as Bimbi, from Frankfurt-am Main, who, scientifically, as is his wont, comes to be absorbed in the new home after first acclimatising himself to the stupefying heat of the Middle East. But his heart remains in Germany, even after spending months in Jerusalem. The story he writes is one of Moses, after he has left Egypt, who, when asked whether he does not miss his original homeland with its developed culture and civilisation, replies that he prefers the potential to the actual. Jerusalem, he writes to his mother, is an "absolute city". The two principal characters of the novel come together when Sarah, Don Amirillo's daughter, starts to work in Heinz's clinic. Together, they ponder the meaning of life and consider how best to conduct themselves, as well as how to apply such conclusions to Medicine, i.e. to the preservation of life. But the effort to preserve life is bound to be frustrated; the most that can be achieved is to postpone death for a while, as he says to the nurses at their graduation.[21] Thus, Medicine is always necessarily provisional, and, in that sense, doomed to failure. This is a fact that those in the profession must recognise. If they do not take this into account, they should be refused permission to practise.

The central family in this novel is in close contact with a wide range of ethnic groups, and they take their close friends from the immigrants, such as Heinz, from amongst the Arabs, such as Subhi Bey and his wife Faiza, as well as from those of their own background. One feature of this novel is the demonstration of how this informal and mutually respectful atmosphere changes over the period of Mandatory rule, with the growing military tensions and the splintering into tight knot and exclusive groups. There is growing antipathy, turning into hostility, between the British, the Arabs and the Jews, who are all beginning to work, exclusively and violently, for their own national interests. These interest are not mutually compatible. The personal has then to give way to the national direction, actual or imagined, and sharp lines increasingly separate one community from another, creating a city of a very different character. The text here reflects the growing tension of the years 1936-1939, known in Arab historiography as "The Arab Revolt". This is the time when virtual civil war reigned between Arabs and Jews on the one hand, and, on the other, between the Jewish settlement and the British, with the protest of the former against the imposition of immigration restrictions on Jews fleeing the increasing persecutions in Europe. This three sided conflict was not to permit the sort of gentle intercourse that had been customary, and was to develop into all out war, with winners and losers, where each party regarded the other as inimical to its own specific interests.

The party that Heinz holds for his friends, in celebration of his success in planting the cedar tree, assumes the aura of a farewell to

---

21. Ibid. p.51.

the old life. In his speech to the assembled company, he announces: Dear friends...I love you all, separately and together. I see this love feast as one of the last corners of culture in the whole world, in which unfortunately, barbarism is increasingly taking hold. I don't know if the next generation will ever have the feeling again that we do today, of comradeliness and friendship.[22] That seems to sum up an era and a mood. Henceforth, all was to change, and degenerate into enmity and factitiousness. Sarah herself senses this at the same party, when she declares to her newly discovered cousin: "'I think that a completely new phase is starting. That we are celebrating some sort of conclusion. There are a lot of tensions here in the city, Eli, even in this garden; we have set them aside today, to celebrate Bimbi, whom we all love. But how long can we carry on setting tensions aside?'"[23] It is as though Jerusalem has a dynamic of its own, which will carry its inhabitants with it, whatever they themselves might happen to want. At the party too, Subhi Bey recognises that a wall has been erected between his own family and their hosts, separating off the ethnic entities and communities.

The development of the story line reflects the increasingly ugly hostilities. There is the anti-British feeling within the *yishuv,* as well as the enmity between Jew and Arab, as it becomes apparent that both parties cannot be satisfied in any post-colonial arrangement. The ethnic divides are sharpened, and the violence increases. Heinz is stabbed and rendered helpless as *jihad* is declared, and the *shabab* (yobs) attack this beloved and humane doctor. Jerusalem is rendered a changed city, with everyone now a soldier in some sort of military setup, declared or otherwise. In the wake of the second world war, at which point the narrative is concluded, we find Sarah again pondering Jerusalem, the city that turns out to be the hero of the novel, the hinge on which all the action is suspended. All the characters in fact revolve around the city, and attempt to grasp it. It seems possible, asserts Sarah, to touch the heavens there now. But the phase conjured up in the prelude is also a time to we all (the characters and perhaps the reader too) would necessarily hark back.

22. Ibid. p.68.
23. Ibid. p.75.

And Yiddish is Dead (or Murdered?)

Aspects of the past that have disappeared for the new Israeli include both a major part of the Jewish people and the language that they have used to communicate their lives, i.e. Yiddish. Together with the murdered six million, there has also disappeared the civilisation that they carried with them. But there is a certain ambivalence in the history of this relationship, an ambivalence which is explored in the novel, *Foiglman*,[24] by the veteran novelist, Aharon Megged. The narrator, Zvi Arbel, a sixty-one year old Israeli historian, opens his story by recalling the death of two people very close to him (in different ways); his wife, Nora, and, shortly afterwards, the Yiddish writer, Foiglman. As an Israeli and a Hebrew writer, Arbel is accused (and self-accused) of being part of an anti Yiddish conspiracy. Is he part of the concerted attempt to wipe out the Yiddish heritage and the residual vestiges of Yiddish culture, through the assertion of the new Israeli identity? The opening marks out the tone of mourning; we have both a personal and a historical loss marked out, as the narrator mourns the situation of the Yiddishist cut adrift by the facts of history. The fact that Arbel is a historian of the Jews seems to make his activity all the more complicit. The reader may be forced to pose the question; is he indeed a mourner or an implicit assassin? The bifurcated stance of the narrator towards the eponymous hero not only crushes him, but also, by implication, makes a statement about Israeli culture.

It seems that there at least two ways of looking back. For Foiglman's son, the father's stance, paradoxically, was nostalgic. He had been preoccupied with the destruction of European Jewry, and had wanted to prepare an exhaustive lexicon of Holocaust material. This was a special sort of nostalgia, a nostalgia even for what is dreadful and horrific, looking back on a time when the Jews had been special, and when consequently they had suffered a "special" fate. For the narrator, one is looking back towards the representation of a culture as well as to the culture itself, and to the people of which he still remains an integral part, although cut off in land and language.

---

24. Aharon Megged, *Foiglman* (Foiglman), Am Oved. Tel Aviv, 1987.

And for the narrator himself as well, there are apparently other ways of looking back, as there are also various ways of not looking back. His own path is to immerse himself in Jewish history, and specifically in the story of persecutions over the last three centuries in Poland. So this is the path of research, uncovering the past patiently and methodically, whilst being motivated by current empathy. But for Foiglman, there is no straining after effects, as he himself, as Yiddish writer and survivor, belongs to that scenario. For the narrator's wife, Nora, and for her family, as well as for Foigman's assimilationist son, this whole Jewish history bit is something to be forgotten, or, preferably perhaps, not known in the first place. The narrator, whose profession illustrates his preoccupations, conducts an extended reflection on the meaning of Jewish history. He investigates how it unfolds, what possibilities it holds old, what directions it might take, and, even, what directions it could have taken. So he is interested not only in what actually happened, but in what could have happened had other decisions been made. Is Jewish history a personal, national and inevitable pattern of unavoidable repetitions? As in Hareven's novel, Nora's mother looks back on a time in Palestine, not so very long ago, when there prevailed a different atmosphere in regard to relations between the communities: "'Those days, in which we could sit together in peace, Jews, Arabs, the English too, will, it seems, never come back.'"[25] So, in the novel, we have a speculation not only on events and history, but on hypothetical possibilities too. Do things change or not within the ongoing saga of the Jews? The recurrent pattern seems to demand a negative response. But, if that be the case, what is our own function as individuals, asks the Israeli, and why have Israel? Foiglman's poetry constitutes some sort of literary response. But others, Foiglman's own son for example, think it kitsch. The Yiddish poet himself sometimes tends towards this view, and asserts this not only of his writing, but of Jewish history altogether; it seems to be kitsch indeed, melodrama. No-one could normally imagine anything so dreadful.

The speculation on the meaning of Jewish history is intertwined with the narrator's own life story. Major aspects of his life at this

---

25. Ibid. p.64.

time include the troubled relationship with his son, Yoav, and the sudden suicide of his wife, astonishing indeed to all who knew her. The focus of the plot, however, is Foiglman himself, and he too serves as a catalyst for the narrator's own understanding of the overall Jewish situation. We see how this sometimes unattractive, nagging figure acts upon the narrator, and, in turn, is acted upon by him. Foiglman becomes the focus of Arbel's attention, and then serves as a symbol of a more general picture, ceasing to be just one single individual, with whom he has by chance come into contact. It is the narrator, Arbel, who plays such a central function in bringing the little known Yiddish poet to the attention of the Hebrew reading public ib Israel. He is even, though perhaps unwittingly, responsible for Foiglman's partial emigration from France to Israel, offering him the opporunity of a new home and an additional readership. Arbel's historiographical speculations can also be seen in the light of the subjection of theory to the test of truth. What, he reflects, is the purpose of writing history? Is it merely to tell the story of the winners, or perhaps the story of the greater number? And if it is generally so regarded, why should a banal body count be the decisive factor in pronouncing significance? Is it only size that counts? All such considerations may play a part in the understanding of the historian, an understanding which can affect Arbel'sattitude towards the Yiddish poet. Is Foiglman a poet of the past, the poet of a defeated minority, of a pathetic and dying breed? On the other hand, is not the historian also a sort of fiction writer, a novelist? However much he may appear to remain faithful to the facts and to documents, does he not also have to make a selection, either through limitations of knowledge and capacity, or through choice and the search for patterns consistent with his own tendencies and imagination?

Foiglman is a novel of encounter, an encounter between the narrator, a professor of Jewish history, and the Jewish past, as well as between himself and the living representative of that past, possessing all of its features, positive and negative. The encounter described is also one between elements of himself and his own accretions, family extensions and the personality that he imprints on the space that he covers. The Israeli State too is part of this meeting, in the way that it has dealt with the past, and the direction that it has selected to navigate. The symbolic war between Yiddish and Hebrew, the substitution of the former for the latter as the dominant modern Jewish language with all the ideological implications entailed, is also embodied in this narrative. Arbel's ambivalence towards Foiglman is an expression, both in personal and ideological terms, of his deeply troubled uncertainty regarding all his material. Foiglman himself is very aware of this ambivalence, as Arbel discovers when he reads the writer's diary. As Arbel's guest in Tel Aviv, the Yiddish poet had been troubled by the lack of a sense of natural communication, despite the forced politeness, and had noted: 'Perhaps I am a "historical document" for him.'[26] The narrator is unable to draw together the various strands of his worlds, and still include within them his wife, Nora, so Nordic, mysterious and ultimately gentile. That could not be integrated into his totality. The tension between the two, the loving couple, is confirmed by her affair in Jerusalem, which either completely shatters her equanimity, or is an expression of an already existing breach. It is this that leads (we presume, we can never be certain) to her disaster, to her despair, to her suicide, and thus to his consequent perplexity. In this novel, disguised as a long memoir, there is also an investigation, conducted by the narrator into his own inner world, as that too acts upon external reality. But it is also a portrait of individuals consumed by guilt. Nora feels guilty because she had been unfaithful, and she now seeks to put an end to her life, so vehemently had she earlier asserted the necessity of absolute integrity. Foiglman's sense of guilt is apparent in his every action and statement. It is spelt out too in his diary and in his account of dreams, where he is reproached by inmates from the camps for some treachery. The narrator's guilt is expressed in the compulsive assistance extended to Foiglman, and in his self sacrifice. Both Nora and Foiglman find the division within themselves unbearable, and this inability to live constitutes the starting point of the novel, from which the narrator embarks on the story. Still, beyond his death, the spirit of Foiglman invades the narrator and the narrative, continually pursuing our devoted but tormented historian.

---

26. Ibid. p.198.

What is Mourning?

It will be evident from this discussion that the intention here is not to impose any sense of pure regret on the view of the past promoted by the fiction described. We are not dealing with a hankering after a lost Eden. The view of the past as evidenced by such novels is by no means sentimental or idealising. In fact, pain and defects are sometimes magnified to grotesque dimensions, and take on mythic properties. But the contemporary narrative here is filtered through the channel of earlier generations, history, geography, faith and aspiration. It is only these elements which enable the present to be structured in words. A peculiar difficulty of Israeli society lies precisely in its lack of continuity over consecutive generations. There is a disjunction to which the authors here are heir. Whether it be the loss of Jewish and Yiddish civilisation in Europe, or the idealistically motivated emigration to Palestine of the founding fathers, there remains a gap to be filled, an imaginative leap to be made in order to recreate the original circumstances of that situation. Only then can the resulting pattern be accommodated into the makeup of the current literary text, relating to Israel and to its people.

A conspectus of Israeli fiction can, in this instance, provide a range of views of the past. In their various ways, the novelists, Shaham, Shalev, Hareven and Megged, so different generationally and aesthetically, have generated a sense of excitement in submitting the past of Israel, ideological and historical, to contemporary inspection. Clearly, no unambiguous conclusions have been drawn. But a number of questions have been raised. Is the past unrecoverable? Is Jewish Fate immutable? Are ideologies of the past or the present valid and helpful? These novels provide us with an exacting measure of a view that unites the various strands of life. This sort of view, inevitably and naturally, derives from the past, but belongs still to the present. What can we make of the Jewish past? Is it a continuum, and, if so, is it a necessary continuum? What is our relationship to the modern Jewish Palestinian revolution, as conducted by the pioneers? What is to be done with our recent memory of the inter-communal relations in the Land, and why have they been so damaged? Must they remain forever impaired? Is this too a necessary concomitant of a particular historical phase? And what are the ideological implications for our overall self-understanding? It is significant that in order to bring the full weight of analysis to bear on the current situation, the Israeli novel, as exemplified in this small sample of work, has attempted, above all else, to understand aspects of the past.

IX

BROKEN NARRATIVE
OF HOLOCAUST REPRESENTATION

Representing the Ineffable

Not everything can be reproduced in words, although verbal language is the major tool for the conveyance of experience. Human communication is of course a very subtle instrument, with a rich and flexible range, that bears an intricate and long history as well as an extensive geographical sweep. Words are symbols, whose letters and sounds may stand in a one to one relationship with the matter represented. But they can also move far beyond being just part of an equation, into realms of suggestion that shade between areas, and they can not easily be cut off from other areas, and confined to a single spot. Physical objects may be relatively easy to represent without ambiguity. You can point to something, and then find a word for it. Thoughts, emotions and ideas though, are, of their nature, intangible, and their character undemonstrable except by analogy and appeal to other words and combinations of words. Verbal complication gets compounded the more that these abstract concepts are involved. Language fights hard and constantly reconstructs itself in the effort to indicate its objective as precisely as possible.

But the strain is considerable. When emotion is taken to the recognisable limit, it may still be contained and conveyed within the existing frame and by familiar means. It would remain a decipherable message. But then the experience behind the word might move further, and eventually extend beyond the orbit of the known and familiar. Words still remain the appropriate, and, in some cases, the sole means of communication available for what must be conveyed. However, they are also inadequate, as they are linked to past, historical usages, based on what has been learned and lived. But what about what has been hitherto unknown? One can not give up on the ambition to render into words; the effort of representation must be made. But the paradox is that verbal and literal authenticity also has to bear the recognition of its own ultimate inadequacy, whilst holding enough charge to point further in the right direction. (The right direction in this case is achievement of its objective, the discovery of a verbal equivalent for feeling). The user of words must recognise the limitations of an unequal medium, and understand that they only move towards the represented experience whilst unavoidably lagging behind it. So, the text must aim to achieve two things; accuracy and tact. It has to be precise, rich and well constructed, but it also has to be silent at the appropriate moment. Silence is, of course, only effective in contrast to the sound that encloses it, but then it can "speak" volumes. This silence is a recognition of the limitation of the word rather than ideal in its own right, and should not be confused with the inadequacy of the pretentious author glorifying in a state that is in actuality merely verbal incompetence.

Representation of the Holocaust experience is a case in point. It has to push language to the limit, as the events and the epoch have no precedent. That experience also surpasses known norms, although there are, as we might expect, familiar elements all along the route. The Holocaust in total is composed of commonly found ingredients; hatred, murder, sadism, barbarity. These though have been ratched up to such a degree, that the total becomes more than a sum of its parts, and eventually becomes unfamiliar. But language is still there, having no option but to meet the challenge posed in finding an adequate context for its verbalisation. This is the theory, the frame, and the content. How to do it is what the post-holocaust writer by implication asks. And the answer is still necessarily to be contained only in the text itself.

Fragments

The disorientation of the individual is captured by Wilkomirski's book, *Fragments.*[1] The narrative of memory is normally linked by continuity of history, a sense of sequence connected by language. But in this case, language has been lost, or perhaps had no chance to exist in the first place, as it was not allowed to develop into mature proportions. The opening words present the problem: 'I have no mother tongue, nor a father tongue either' (3). There had been 'a Babel-babble' overlaying his original Yiddish, derived from the children's barracks in the death camps. This had consisted of a limited language confined to bare essentials, and was replaced by later acquired languages. But those newer accretions were not perceived as his own: 'They were only imitations of other people's speech' (4).

With the loss of an initial, broken and inadequate speech, a substitute had to be found and restored. The past is there, somewhere, so how can it be recaptured? In addition to the aural sense that absorbs verbal language, there is also the visual capacity that leaves its imprint on the memory. These sights are accompanied by feelings and sensations: 'My early childhood memories are planted, first and foremost, in exact snapshots of my photographic memory and in the feelings imprinted in them, and the physical sensations.'(4) This is the primal layer of a past existence linking up to the present effort of recall. Only later comes the memory of things heard. In the mean-time, present and past are jumbled, as can be appropriate in a work about a past, dormant for fifty years, and only now pieced together for the first time. The author has to make sense of the fragmented and suppressed memory of a brutal betrayal by the adult world. This can only with great difficulty be correlated with the stuttering attempts of the post-war onlookers to compensate the emotionally starved and cheated child. So unassimilable is the experience of the child's past that, in order to assimilate and recapture it, it had to be broken up into small, disconnected parts, "fragments", as in the title of the

---

1. Benjamin Wilkomirski, *Fragments.* Picador. London, 1996. Translated from the German by Carol Brown Janeway, originally published in 1995. See also above, cap. 7.

book, or "shards of recollection" (26), as he describes them. These are so different from the normal stream of memory, which should be suggestive and inviting. These, his own recollections, repel and terrorise. "Shards" are dangerous and disconcerting, warning anyone approaching to stay away, and the negative allusion is contained in the use of the word here.[2]

The difficulty of representation is the subject of the book. There is an initial bestiality, now apparently departed. But the past has left a residue that is the only one retained by the child, now maturing, whose fundamental experience was the Holocaust. His life had been a reaction to hatred, to the overwhelming need to kill and to the deprivation of any protective layer. It must only be inevitable that the "other" takes its representation from that initial experience. Even the kindly Mrs. Grosz, who is to bring him to a peaceful and prosperous Switzerland, is seen as alien, someone belonging to another sphere, speaking a strange, although somewhat similar tongue. It was, after all, betrayal by adults, so misleading and contrary, that had led him into disaster initially. It was a well dressed woman who seemed to bear authority, control and promise, who in fact transported him to Majdanek. She had promised to reunite the lost and disorientated child with his brothers. And, as he discovered after realisation of the deceipt, the "gray lady" was lying. 'Majdanek is no playground.'(37) At this new venue, the child collides head on with another reality, and he is plunged into a constant state of terror. This is a place of

---

2. The discussion here is conducted on the basis of the book as it stands, as a piece of literature, and as a work that presents itself as documentary history and memoir. It seems that the book is not based on the author's own experiences, but that these are incorporated into the works as though they were his own actual biography. This discovery was made initially by Daniel Ganzfried, and published in the Swiss paper, *Weltwoche*, at the end of August, 1998. According to Ganzfried, Wilkomirski was in fact Bruno Desker, born in Switzerland out of wedlock, and later adopted by a wealthy Swiss couple, and that he has lived in Switzerland all his life. Apparently, Wilkomirski later argued that he has always allowed the reader of his book to treat ir as work of imagination and empathy. For a discussion of this issue see the article by Ilana Hammerman: "'Hashem hayah yafeh: tarbut hashoah vehazikaron.' *Haaretz*, 4 December, 1998. See also the report in the London Times, 8 September, 1998, p.12, 'Testimony of Holocaust "survivor" denounced as fiction', which relates the controversy to the issue of Holocaust denial and the importance of reliable testimony.

aggressive dogs, of rats, and disgusting bugs, in fact, of lurking death.

But the rules acquired for survival in the concentration camp are inimical to the new environment of the Swiss orphanage. Here, he tries to apply the lessons he has initially absorbed. He is now on continual alert, awaiting retribution, for example, for snatching at the food which seems to be available in such abundance. But everyone knows, do they not, that apparent goodies may be just as suddenly removed? That is what his life experience has taught him. The book cuts between the two venues, and criss-crosses the impressions. You cannot learn the contrary just by being informed of it. He had been told of the contrary before, at the formative point of his life, that which was also crucial in his makeup. This had brought about the loss of his family, friends, mentors, environment, country and language. So in order to comprehend the total personality we have to see the operative factors in its composition. We have to see the picture both ways; Majdanek in the light of Switzerland, but Switzerland too in the light of Majdanek. Can the two faces of the Janus be reconciled? Perhaps such a reconciliation is inconceivable and indeed impossible, but at least the two aspects can be aware, each one of the other, as between the covers of a single volume. A single, complete literary work must be a unity, and thus contain the elements of oneness.

And yet, although the parts of the narrator's experience seem to contradict each other, and to remain totally separate, each constantly invades the space of the other. In the incident of the missing shoes, when they seem to have disappeared from his locker, he is forcibly reminded of the disaster of his shoes lost at the camp. To lose one's shoes in a concentration camp is one of the worst things that can happen to you. So this sets off a panic in the new environment, as his consciousness crashes back in time. And yet, his shoes, which had been soaked in the rain, had only been removed by the nurse to dry off. This had given rise to much ribaldry amongst the other children, whose life experience had been so different from his, that they could just as well have come from some distant planet. His time at the orphanage is lived in the shadow of the earlier existence. This phase of his life is by no means dead. It is not even completely overshadowed, but just waiting, cunningly to return and to reassert itself.

Human behaviour is paradoxical and unexpected according to a utilitarian logic. We might expect that one who has passed through such horrifying experiences would only wish to obliterate them from his memory. To some extent, indeed, that is what happens as long as the pleasure principle reigns.[3] We have seen that for many years, the author has apparently managed to sweep that other life under the carpet, and it may well be that that path was the only one that enabled him to survive, just literally and physically to maintain his own life. To bear the awareness of that past whilst confronting a new reality might well have rendered him incapable of functioning. But fifty years after the events, another principle takes over, in the exquisitely painful process of the attempt to recapture the past. And we also see that in the immediate aftermath of the war too, the child was attempting to move back. However great the horror, he was drawn to it more than to the uncharted territory of the alluring comforts apparently on offer. There was something in this recent desolation that made it particularly his own, and he was concerned to move on his own ground. He writes about the period shortly after being taken to the orphanage: 'Again and again I thought back through all my memories. I didn't want to lose or forget anything, because I wanted to run away from here. I wanted to get back somehow. I thought the only way I'd find my way back would be if I remembered every place, every street, every house, and every barracks.'(67) We have indeed moved beyond the pleasure principle to the search for that initial source of pain and terror. If we would want to know why he apparently pursues this nightmare, he offers the suggestion: 'I could only get away from this unbearable strange present by going back to the world and the images of my past. Yes, they were almost unbearable, but they were familiar, at least I understood their rules.' (68)

---

3. According to Freud, the pleasure principle is the logical norm and the dominant principle in human life and aspiration. The normal core of events involves the lowering of tension, he argues. However, this direction might be inhibited, and that is when we move 'beyond the pleasure principle.' See Sigmund Freud, *Jenseits des Lustprinzips.* Leipzig, 1920. (English translation) *Beyond the Pleasure Principle.* London, 1922.

That horror is locked into his mind at the primal stage, and has become his home, however unpleasant and painful. Indeed, the descriptions of the camp are so numbing that they are virtually unbearable for the reader, let alone for the subject. We have for example, piles of starving but still living infants tossed into the dormitory that he occupied. They were not to remain alive for long. Horrors previously unimaginable are realised here in living biography. Murder is a constant presence, wholesale, arbitrary and indifferent. This is a world in which the process of immediate and sudden death is the norm, a world in which women have to die once they have had children (85). They also appear to be giving birth to rats (86). It would seem that the situation could not get worse when he then finds himself tossed into a huge mound of corpses. The child's survival is only assured by a miraculous escape into a women's camp, where he is hidden and protected against enormous odds.

The evident end of the war is not clearly marked by the child's consciousness. Strange events indeed come about, when he is taken, by an unknown woman who recognises him, back to Kraków of all places, that place where his miserable journey had started. A life had been going on outside of which he knew nothing, and he has to learn everything anew. Frau Grosz is the herald of another world called Switzerland, where he is to be moved, but of which he is violently suspicious. The adults talk of transport, but the child thinks that he knows what that means, and he screams in terror. His apparent salvation leaves him with a sense of his own treachery, that he has abandoned those to whom he truly belonged. It would take years before he could really trust anyone else. So, for him, the war does not end in 1945, but just moves on into a new phase. There is constant misunderstanding between the child and his environment, as those around attempt to acclimatise him to normality. But he is full of fear and guilt. The Swiss legend of William Tell, with which he is confronted at school, is for the child, just another story of a brutal soldier shooting at children. His behaviour is conditioned by his past and is not amenable to the soothing interpretation now placed upon this new environment.

Even growing up now in Switzerland, those intial feelings persist, and accompany him into adulthood. He now energetically refutes what he regards as the myth of the end of the war, and the "liberation". There was, for him, no such liberation in the sense shown on newsreels and films. His memory of that episode is quite different. He is entreated to forget his own memory, and that sort of betrayal, as he sees it, he rejects. He still regards the apparent good life on offer as a trap in disguise, awaiting a suitable opportunity to spring on its unsuspecting prey. He is even forced to doubt himself and the truth of his own memory and experience: 'Perhaps it's true - somehow I missed my own liberation.' (152) Wilkomirski's book is an attempt to find himself once more, and to convince himself as well as others of his own authenticity: 'I wrote these fragments of memory to explore both myself and my earliest childhood; it may also have been an attempt to set myself free.' (155) This is from the later summary in the "afterword" to the book.

The special reality of that other time and place is the only one recognised, and it subsumes all others, even when those seem to obtrude. The book takes us in both directions, to the distant past, the more recent past, and then the present, until they permeate each other. But one can be mistaken in one's assumptions. The present can be a disguise for an apparently censored past. Mila was a girl he knew at the camp, whom he meets again later in life, as an adult, when she was working as a translator and he as a musician: 'Mila and I saw each other regularly now – we often had long talks. We discussed the present, but what we really meant was our past. Both of us were living among the living, yet we didn't really belong with them - we were actually the dead, on stolen leave, accidental survivors who got left behind in life.' (82) That residue from the other time was so much more potent than the surface reality that it did not allow it to breathe. And yet, it was also so formidable that it prohibited penetration. The love that the two held for each other '[w]as always accompanied by a fear of touching what actually bound us together.' (82) This leads then to another loss, and they part, as they can not go forward, and they are also terrified of going back. That means that they can only part company. Aspects of normal; natural life become confused in his mind with images of the camp, so that even the healthy birth of his own child becomes a source of nausea (88).

Broken Narrative as the Contemporary Fiction

It is not only difficult to characterise such a work as *Fragments* and to assign it an appropriate generic definition; it may also be that this difficulty is itself an integral part of the work's makeup. The book is clearly not presented as a work of "fiction" (an invented narrative). We see that the story purports to render as faithful an account as possible of the actual events pertaining to the narrator's childhood, as viewed from a considerable distance of time. Thus it is, to this degree, a memoir, conveying factuality, as well as its accompanying sentiment. This emotion is naturally though also the story itself. And so is the problematic nature of the telling. The telling becomes the narrative; the thorny nature of the rendition of straight truth becomes the text before us. The objective material sought by the teller is intimately bound up with such subjective factors as memory and obfuscation. The memory is necessarily imperfect anyway, but here the defective memory is a tool of survival. It is only later that recovery is seen to be possible only in the process of recall.

This may be a paradox, and one that can lead us to discern the lineaments of a new type of fiction. For the most part, the memorial writer has to engage in a process of sifting. So overwhelming usually is the abundance of the material that the writer must needs edit, cut down and reduce to manageable proportions in order to exercise some degree of control. The issue there is not so much what to include, but rather what to leave out in order to allow the principal features to emerge. For the maker of such a document as *Fragments,* however, the difficulty is the reverse. Instead of skimming off from an over abundant stock, he has to build it up. Almost everything has disappeared, or, at least, been submerged. What Freud described as the "magic writing pad of memory"[4] has been left blank by the necessity of a cruel life, and the writer now must needs recreate it. But he

---

4. Sigmund Freud, "Notiz über der 'Wunderblock'", 1925 ("A Note upon the 'Mystic Writing Pad'"). The memory works rather like this pad, according to Freud. It can retain impressions, but, for reasons of practicality as it does not want to store too much material, especially if that material seems to be discardable and irrelevant in the long run, it can also wipe out parts in order to make way for the new. So the memory fulfills both functions, both retaining and replacing.

must still do it whilst remaining faithful to the discharge of his duty, that is, to the truth. Otherwise, there is no point in the overall exercise. In order to achieve this, he produces a different sort of order from what is most common in narrative writing. That traditional mode is based on sequence of event, things told in the order of their occurrence. Primo Levi too declared this different approach,[5] which would be based on strands of impression and the way that they fall on the mind of the diarist, rather than on chronological sequence. Factuality here is also the way in which the mind can be bent in the service of this recall in order to preserve the basic elements of truth. In sum, a disjointed subject should also, in this view, bring about a disjointed text. Otherwise, it is a text not true to its own subject and purpose. The author aspires not just to present the facts of his life, which objective might in any case be better served by other, more reliable means, but the feeling behind it. And that feeling is broken up, shattered into "shards", and awaiting if not an impossible restoration, at least a more informed assessment.

Fugitive Pieces

The title of the novel by Anne Michaels[6] bears a remarkable and coincidental resemblance to the book by Wilkomirski. The term "fugitive pieces" sounds rather like "fragments", and both bear the sense of pieces broken off from a larger whole, the major part of which is unavailable or has disappeared. In both works then, there is a suggestion that there is a larger story to tell, but that since the conveyor of the tale is an imperfect subject buffeted by misfortune and inevitable memory loss, the story will be built up gradually and imperfectly. A further suggestion might be that it could well be supplemented at a later stage, and also that the book in its present

---

5. In the author's preface to his first major work, *Se questo è un uomo*. Ennaudi. Torino, 1958 (*If this is a Man*. Translated by Stuart Woolf. Penguin Books. London, 1979), there is an "apology" for the "fragmentary character" of the book. Levi asserts that '[t]he chapters have been written not in logical succession, but in order of urgency.'

6. Anne Michaels, *Fugitive Pieces*. Bloomsbury. London, 1996.

form is only provisional. Negatively, this could be regarded as defective, but, positively, this could be taken as a virtue, an admission that it is the subject who is the container, and, that to admit to the limitations of such a narrative, is also a mark of its honesty and faithfulness to the matter that it seeks to convey. Both deal with Holocaust material, that is, with a horrendous subject which those who have experienced it might well prefer to suppress, if possible. Indeed, this act of suppression or, at the least, repression,[7] might well be a precondition for the ability to live normally and to function successfully. How can one live with the persistent consciousness of that dreadful history?

Fugitive Pieces purports to be the memoir of the poet, Jakob Beer, who survived his childhood in occupied Poland, and later died in Athens in 1993. So here we perhaps have the key to the generic distinction made between the two works, *Fragments* and *Fugitive Pieces*. The former purports to be a memoir by the author himself, whereas the latter contains a memoir. So the former is described as "non-fiction"[8], whereas the latter is categorised as a novel. But the overall thrust of the two books is quite similar. Both are very delayed accounts of the events of the war. In fact, the account by Beer is said to be interrupted by his death at the age of sixty, and is thus incomplete, even in the intention of the memoirist, quite apart from the nature of its inherent incompleteness. Both recognise the damage inflicted by those events on the subjective consciousness, and thus on narrative reliability. But both also testify to the necessity of recognising this partiality and of recording it as the unfiltered testimony of experience. In both then, the time lapse between experience and transmutation into a narrative account, is of the essence of the work. Both works raise the question of how to memorialise. They recognise the problem, but still assert the value of a limited representation, which is superior both to no representation at all, and also to an inauthentic representation that would not bear such scars of imperfection.

---

7. Suppression is conscious, repression unconscious in psychoanalytic understanding. See Charles Rycroft, *A Critical Dictionary of Psychoanalysis.* Penguin Books. London, 1972.
8. It won the *Jewish Quarterly* award for non-fiction in the year of its publication. It was later withdrawn in the belief that it was not factually based.

Jakob Beer's memoir, the story within a story, opens with confusion, with emergence from the mud. The world that has been is no more. His is a story, whose origins are obscure, and the carrier of which can not really follow through, back to its origins: 'I did not witness the most important events of my life. My deepest story must be told by a blind man, a prisoner of sound.' (17) Now, Beer attempts to summon up the nightmare of intrusion, attack, slaughter of his family, and his own flight. The language used tries to capture the disjointed, dream like nature of the experience, remote from human intercourse and urban living, a world of threatening nature, the forest, the bog, a child isolated, in flight and terror. Human communication is also a remote attribute, and the only phrase he knows in more than one language is "dirty Jew", a phrase he repeats about himself, to point to himself in conveying his identity to others, beating his own chest. This is how he communicates to Athos, the man excavating, who finds him. It is Athos who saves the seven year old Jakob, taking him to the Greek island of Zakynthos, to hide and protect him. His arrangement could hold the key to a new existence, and to the forgetting of the past, to its ultimate consignment: 'I longed to cleanse my mouth of memory. I longed for my mouth to feel my own when speaking his beautiful and awkward Greek, its thick consonants, its many syllables difficult and graceful as water rushing around rock.' (22) Lives are lived separately, but in parallel lines, coming together unexpectedly, as the lineage of the two is distant but mutually resonant. Beer, the narrator, may contain more of the distant past than of the present. This is noted by Athos, who, as the interlocutor, also serves as Beer's mirror, and tells him: '"Sometimes I can't look you in the eye; you're like a building that's burned out inside, with the outer walls still standing."' (30) Beer is literally a shell of a person after what he has traversed, and he finds the remote past more accessible than what had happened just a very few years back. But the community of Athos too had been, and remained later, in Greece as well, still under threat. They had saved each other, when Biskupin had been abandoned, and Athos's colleagues transported to Dachau. (51) The strange symbiosis between adult and child, between Greek and Jew, is also responsible for the preservation of more than Beer himself, as Beer holds within him his beloved sister, Bella. He has become the repository of the family and of the clan. The child now carries within himself a responsibility beyond himself, and he has to search out a suitable destiny, as well as the means for its realisation. Merely to survive is not sufficient; you have to know where to go:'To survive was to escape fate. But if you escape your fate, whose life do you then step into?' (48) Beer's account looks for an answer to just this question. It is indeed a question that could be put to everyone. But for one such as Beer, this question has an insistent and striking application that can not be avoided in his peculiar and shocking circumstances. The thrust of the main character, supported by his interlocutor, and given a frame by the narrator, is a search for meaning in a world that must be contrasted with the moral vacuum inherited and now superseded. He is tormented by the problem of memorialisation. The problem is indeed imponderable and intractable: 'How can one man take on the memories of even one other man, let alone five or ten or a thousand or ten thousand; how can they be sanctified each?' (52) The question is left hanging in the air, as the narrative continues into the post-war phase. The principal preoccupation of Athos, and indeed of the whole book, is memory. He wants to know how the past can be perpetuated by the present living, and how the living can ensure their own perpetuity. He encourages Beer to memorialise his family as well as those who have no family to recall them, and he instils the need to ensure his own memorialisation. He tells him, on the eve of their journey to Canada, after the war: ' "Jakob, try to be buried in the ground that will remember you." '(76)

Still in Greece, in hiding and protected by his mentor, the geologist Athos, Beer is encouraged to remember his past. And, as in geology, the process of remembering involved is a form of rediscovery, digging deep to bring to the surface materials unseen and not perceived by the conscious mind. He is taught to relearn the Hebrew alphabet, as well as the shape of the Greek letters and the sounds of the ancient Greek language. The source of identity, he learns, lies behind, beneath and beyond what we immediately apprehend. This latter, i.e. that which comes easily to mind, belongs just to the surface, whereas there is a greater reality disdainful of our own transient and changing perceptions and opinions. He tells Athos, when grown up of course, that his Jewishness is just there, rock solid at his base whatever he might think of it: ' "But Athos, whether one believes or not has nothing to do with being a Jew. Let me put it this way: The truth doesn't care what we think of it." ' (107) But he also aspires to transcend language, to find his own truth in a primal system, the property of humankind wherever and whenever, to which specific language is a later and imperfect key. Athos himself had recognised this in others. For example, his friend, Kostas never mentioned his late wife, Helen: ' "Some stones are so heavy only silence helps you carry them." ' (77) Memorialisation through the process of articulation is, as we have noted above, not always, possible or conceivable. But Beer still strives to find the appropriate tone. Athos had told him: ' "In a foreign landscape, a man discovers the old songs." ' (86) He begins to find himself by the recall of a past made urgent by exile. And in Toronto, he tries to achieve it: 'I listened to these dark shapes as if they were black spaces in music, a musician learning the silences of a piece. I felt this was my truth. That my life could not be stored in any language, but only in silence; the moment I looked into the room and took in what was visible, not vanished. The moment I failed to see Bella had disappeared.' (111) There is an ongoing struggle between articulation and silence, between the act of verbalisation and the recognition that it is not possible. Silence is his own preferred and ideal mode, but that too is seen to be beyond his reach. His aim is to '[i]solate that space, that damaged chronology in words, in an image, then perhaps one could restore order by naming.' (111) When Athos dies, Beer takes him back to Greece, the land that would remember him, and Jakob sees it as his function to try to complete his unfinished work.

As for Jakob, everything that has been, still remains, and it retains its permanent imprint. In spite of his new life and his enthusiasm for the present, for his poetry, for his exciting wife, Alexandra, Bella, the sister of his past, is still with him So are the Jews of Poland, so horrifyingly murdered together with their culture. He stays out of Alexandra's very contemporary life so as not to spoil her fun. ' "You'll have a better time without me" '(145), he tells her. Eventually, she leaves him. She has found someone else, and he returns to Greece to find the traces of Athos once more. But this is also an act of self discovery. He quotes a Rabbi who teaches: '[n]othing erases the immoral act.' (160) And: 'History is the poisoned well, seeping into the groundwater.' (161) Everything is for ever retained, the evils as well as the good: 'Destruction doesn't create a vacuum, it simply transforms presence into absence.' (161) This doctrine is totalitarian and unforgiving, as nothing can be obliterated. As Jakob does not believe in death, the poetry that he writes is characterised by someone else as "ghost stories" (163), as the dead figures are still present. The past is also the future; his son by his beloved Michaela, his chosen companion, will be Bela, if male, or Bella, if female (194). Michaela is the antithesis of himself, the epitome of life. It is with her that he can know the colour of yellow, which he had not hitherto experienced: 'The first morning I woke to Michaela – my head on the small of her back, her heels like two islands under the blanket – I knew that this was my first experience of the colour yellow.' (184) There are forces around that aspire to bring him back to life, but perhaps Alexandra's power had been too tenuous, and Michaela will work from within his own world. It is clear that the most intimate area of himself is that occupied by Bella, the two syllables that will constitute his child's name. This is the object of his yearning.

In the second part of the novel, the narrator, Ben,[9] meeting Beer, ponders the nature of biography. He discovers that his own apparent interest in archaeology is a disguise for his concern with biography.(221) He must imagine who these distant people were and are, for they still exist in the present. The quest of archaeology is the quest expressed in biography, which is that of love: 'The quest to discover another's psyche, to absorb another's motives as deeply as your own, is a lover's quest.' (222) That quest goes beyond the search for facts: 'But the search for facts, for places, names, influential events, important conversations and correspondences, political circumstances – all this amounts to nothing if you can't find the assumption your subject lives by.' (222) We might draw the conclusion that such an assertion holds good not just for biography, but

---

9. He is called Ben (Hebrew for son), as his parents wanted to avoid giving him a full name in the hope that, in this way, the angel of death would pass him by. Two previous children had already been murdered by the Nazis. This is a secret kept from Ben by his parents, and only confided to his wife, Naomi. See *Fugitive Pieces*, p.252.

inevitably then, for fiction too. The subject of fiction, and of books in general, is people. Writing is the work of investigation into the fundamental assumptions of its subjects. The more extraordinary the framework, as in the case of the Holocaust, as well as what preceded and what followed it, the more necessary is the search for these assumptions.

What is in and What is out

The literature relating to the Holocaust, in order to merit its venerated appellation, must steer a very difficult course between two currents. One current is the insistence on total expression, the belief that everything contains the potential of one to one representation, that all can be held by the language used. The other current is the impulse towards silence, the belief that what is to be stated can not in fact be stated, as it goes beyond human language, and would be desecrated by the search for a container in the historically tried modes. There is clearly some validity in both directions and tendencies. Literature must be as expressive as possible; that is its function, and, as readers, we believe that it is a worthwhile function. So the language must struggle towards ultimate perfection, the right expression for the required meaning. On the other hand, what about the experience of the unprecedented when it dons the apparel of what is old? Does language not then lamentably fail in its task since it suggests by the means at its disposal that what is being said now is about what has gone before? Does the traditional usage of existing materials not also bear the implication that it is dealing with basically the same material?

It has been suggested that the literature of representation is confronting a crisis in modern times, and that this is due to the peculiarly horrific turn that world history has taken. This crisis hinges on the inadequacy of language to match the experience that it seeks to engage. The function of literature as a quintessentially "literary" activity is to cast fresh light on human experience through the use of language that is both appropriate and fresh. If it is not appropriate, then it is not literary, and if it is not fresh, it might just as well not be written. George Steiner has written: 'The imagination has supped its full of horrors and of the unceremonious trivia through which modern horror is often expressed. As rarely before, poetry is tempted by silence.'[10] Language has suffered from overuse, and desended into repetitious abstraction or unthought cliché. Steiner argues that the language of literature since the seventeenth century, (up to which time it was possible to master the whole range of available knowledge in all disciplines), has inhabited a narrower domain than it did before. Once, literature sought to offer the equivalent of the whole man, of total human experience. But in the age of specialisation, an age where this phenomenon of the fragmentation of knowledge and learning is continually becoming more apparent and getting more extreme, the ambitions of literature have been occupying a more limited area. The reason for this may be that speech lies at the base of what is human, and what we have confronted in the modern age, to some degree what is quintessential to it, goes beyond the human. We must say that if literature attempts to ignore what has happened, it will become trivial, and can then be considered as marginal, or even irrelevant in the larger scheme of things. If, on the other hand, it makes the effort to represent the experience adequately through its traditional medium, that of language, it would have difficulty in finding the appropriate garb. This may be one of the reasons that we find that literature in recent times is experimenting with other modes, and looking for additional, or even substituted, materials in its efforts at memorialisation. Perhaps pictures, photographs, notes, diaries, drawings, or whatever can come to hand, will not undergo, at least collectively, the same restraints and constrictions. Even just the effort itself to search for other forms can allude to the crisis and thus the difference. There is too an additional aspect to the use of photographs. They can be seen not only as ways into the past, into what has already happened, but as a clue to the future as well. Ben, in *Fugitive Pieces*, says: ' "We think of photographs as the captured past. But some photographs are like DNA. In them you can read your whole future." ' (251-2) They have a magical capacity not just to capture a passing moment, but to hold eternity. There are no

---

10. George Steiner, *Language and Silence*. Penguin Books. London, 1967, p.25.

reproductions of photographs in the book, but a great deal of discussion of them.

Holocaust literature must aspire to recognition of two levels of truth, to what is common to human experience overall, and to what is distinctive. The historical experience is that of human beings, people as they have been before, and as they always have been in potential. We must recognise their human traits in whatever they do. What has happened here has traces and sometimes even precise models in earlier events. Language has emerged from that, and this is what must be used. On the other hand, we are dealing here with what is in many significant aspects a unique event. It is a truism that every experience, like every person, is unique. But the Holocaust is cumulatively unique, in its scope, its violence, its assumptions, in what it attempted to do, and in what it suggests about human nature. So the tools of its expression should seek to match that quality, and be correspondingly different. The expression rendered will confront a chasm; language will meet silence, and that should come at the right moment. The two elements have to be combined in the proportions that lend to their maximum efficacy, which is the achievement of the effect sought shaped with authenticity. That is what these two works, *Fragments* and *Fugitive Pieces*, seek to achieve.

Remembering what is not there

Much of the discussion here has centred on the appropriate representation of things as they are. A word or phrase stands for experience in relationship of equivalence, and the problem is to find the proper form of words, and then to craft them in context. But there is another, although seemingly opposite, problem. In the texts before us, there is an effort to recapture what had been there that had apparently disappeared from conscious recall. This has to be hewn out from a covering rock, following a prolonged effort and struggle. Such is the supposed direct burden of *Fragments* and the indirect narrative of *Fugitive Pieces*. In the former, the author is his own narrator and subject, and the book is the fruit, not completely ripe in all respects, of a labour that is seen also as basic therapy.

We have had occasion to note the use made in narratives, not only of photographic representations, which by their nature record events and people that were present, but also the indication of gaps. A space can tell a story, if it is enclosed by the bracketing of a precursor, on the one hand, and, then material subsequent. The gap can speak eloquently in a text too. In fact, the gap can become the tragic subject for the memorialist who has no direct access to the object of mourning.[11] As the narrator writes at the beginning of *Fugitive Pieces*: 'The shadow past is shaped by everything that never happened. Invisible, it melts the present like rain through karst.' (17) There are two negatives here; the past, which is a shadow, i.e. not the thing itself, but an imitation of reality, and "everything", which never happened, which did not occur, and which was yet responsible for everything else. Paradoxically, it does not follow the event, as we might expect of a shadow, whose nature is to come in the wake of the object on which it is dependent. On the contrary, it "foreshadows" it. The shadow in this instant can also be the thing that was not there in historical and physical actuality, but which might have been present for the person who perceives it, as it had been for others. It is the space that is lacking, and is now imaged in outline. So it seems that the most significant things in our history are not objectively present, or, at least, are not there for us to see. And this is the paradoxical sense of silence in literature, the medium of words. Both of our texts have emerged from silence, and they still contain a great deal of it.

---

11. See Marianne Hirsch, "Past Lives: Postmemories in Exile" in Susan Rubin Suleiman, ed. *Exile and Creativity*. Duke University Press. Durham, 1998, p.420: 'For survivors who have been separated and exiled from a ravaged world, memory is necessarily an act not only of recall, but also of mourning, a mourning often inflected by anger, rage and despair.' In spite of the lack of a direct knowledge of the lost world, there still remains, through family and tribal connections and associations, something akin to memory, which the author terms "postmemory". For her: 'photography [i]s precisely the medium connecting memory and postmemory.' (ibid. p. 429).

X

EPILOGUE
PERSPECTIVES FOR THE PAST AND FUTURE

Literature of Crisis in the Twentieth Century

The matter investigated here is the way in which literature creates itself anew in the wake of the changing public scene. Not that literature reflects events, but that a different consciousness emerges when a fundamental reorientation in our view of the world comes about. This does not apply in reaction to specific events of the everyday, even when these are very major or disastrous, but rather when a radical change poses a challenge to previously held assumptions. This rethink invites a rewrite, not only of the material itself, but of the manner of its presentation. In this way new literary movements are born.

We see this with the effect of the repositioning of the Jew in the reorientation that occurred in the life of the people. Until the late nineteenth century, Poland, and some other centres of Eastern Europe that came to constitute the Pale of Settlement, had, for a very long time, constituted the principal centre of Jewish life, in terms of numbers and strength of organisation. But increasing poverty, population explosion, rising national consciousness, pogroms and revolution changed all that. Socialism and Zionism emerged, drawing the ideologically conscious Jews in different directions. A reborn Jewish nationalism attracted a growing element to the ancient homeland of Palestine, with its romantic, religious, historical and ethnic associations, and one of its epi-manifestations was the revival of a language and culture. Anti-Semitism gave birth to a more specifically Jewishly orientated literature amongst writers well established in the various language groups too, as we have seen in the case of Edmond Fleg. The increasing waves of violence and pogroms spawned forms of Expressionism. And, above all, the Holocaust drove the Jewish writer to search out appropriate modes of articulation, in keeping with the unprecedented horror.

Jewish Culturalism and Residual Judaicity

So much had changed for the Jews by the turn of the century. Whether in lands under Islamic rule or within the Christian world, Jews, as a collective, but, following that, individually as well, had been largely defined and shaped by their life within their own contained communities. One of the features that marked out the effects of Emancipation and Enlightenment was the cultural assimilation into a secular environment, a by product of the social intermingling. So an element of choice came increasingly to the fore. The Jews of the twentieth century have become an integrated part of the larger communities in Russia, France, Italy, Germany et al. But, as we well know, this has been a slow, ongoing and unsteady progression, accompanied in their reception by rejection, atavism, resurgence of hostile chauvinism and ethnic, exclusivist loyalties.

The Literature of Crisis

The writing that has accompanied this process has been particularly exciting. Not only is it an expression of its own immediate environment, but it also often evinces the existence of roots elsewhere and echoes beyond. The production of Jewishly conscious writers almost certainly belongs to at least two places. It is at the cutting edge of experimentation. New forms are created or adapted in the service of the repositioning involved in the shift. It is pointless to ask whether a particular body of work has its place within the Jewish world, or whether it belongs more to the national literature of the language in which it is written. It is indeed located in both contexts, and so it is both Jewish and national (of whatever group). Such an outcome also has the effect of blurring the boundaries between the two, and modifying the definitions of each. Crisis calls for adequate articulation, and this search produces the kind of literature presented here.

But there still remain two major directions in which this literature has moved. One has been the pursuit of a resurgent Jewish expression in Jewish languages in the formation of a specifically Jewish culture. This we have witnessed in the nascent Hebrew literature of Palestine/Israel, and in the new Yiddish writing of Eastern Europe, particularly Poland and the USSR. The second direction is that of the body of work dressed in all the predominant European languages which Jewish writers have adopted or into which they were born.

We have not attempted to impose an artificial unity on this totality of work, or to make a discriminatory judgment between the tendencies. As we continue to stress; any faithful presentation of the literature must recognise the various strands and the different cultural traditions, as well as the rival ideologies. And these differences should be seen for what they are, without distortion or imposition of an externally imposed view. But nevertheless, in all its variety, difference and separateness, there remains in some sense a Jewish body of literature, perhaps shifting and ungraspable, but still part of a larger whole. This literature is part of Jewish history, broadly seen and interpreted. But as a literature, it tells its own story too, a story of literary codes, genres, modes and values.

SELECT BIBLIOGRAPHY

Ahad Haam (Asher Ginzberg). *Al parashat drakhim.* 4 volumes. Jüdischer Verlag. Berlin, 1921.

Appelfeld, A. *Bagay haporeh.* Schocken. Tel Aviv, 1963.

Appelfeld, A. *Shanim veshaot.* Hakibbutz hameuhad. Tel Aviv, 1975.

Appelfeld, A. *Masot beguf rishon.* The Zionist Library. Jerusalem, 1979.

Appelfeld, A. *Katerina.* Keter. Jerusalem, 1990.

Appelfeld, A. *Ad sheyaaleh hashahar.* Keter. Jerusalem, 1995.

Appelfeld, A. *Mikhreh haqerah.* Keter. Jerusalem, 1997.

Appelfeld, A. *Sipur hayim.* Keter. Jerusalem, 1999.

Baron, S. *The Russian Jew under Tsars and Soviets.* Macmillan. 2nd. ed. New York, 1976.

Barthes, R. *Le Plaisir du Texte.* Editions du Seuil. Paris, 1973.

Berlowitz, Y. *Lehamtsiy erets lehamtsiy am; sifrut haaliyah harishonah,* Hakibbutz hameuhad. Tel Aviv, 1996.

Defoe, D. *A Journal of the Plague Year.* Originally published anonymously in 1722.

Elbaz, Andre E. ed. *Correspondence d'Edmond Fleg pendant l'affaire Dreyfus.* Libraire A.G.Nizet. Paris, 1976.

Eliav, M. *Sefer haaliyah harishonah.* 2 Vols. Yad Izhak Ben-Zvi. Jerusalem, 1981.

Fleg, E. *Le Trouble-Fête.* Libraire Théâtrale. Paris, 1913.

Fleg, E. *Pourquoi je suis juif.* Les Belles Lettres. Paris, 1995. First published, 1927.

Fleg, E. *Ma Palestine*. Fondation Sefer. Paris, 1932.

Fleg, E. *Jésus raconté par le juif errant*. Albion Michel. Paris, 1953. First published, 1932.

Fleg, E. *Le problème d'aujourd'hui*. Fondation Sefer. Paris, 1948.

Fleg, E. *Anthologie juive: des origines à nos jours*. Flammarion. Paris, 1951.

Frankel, J. *Prophecy and Politics: Socialism, Nationalism and the Russian Jews, 1862-1917*. Cambridge University Press. Cambridge, 1981.

Freud, S. *Jenseits des Lustprizips*. Leipzig, 1920.

Gary, R. *La Danse de Genghis Cohn*. Gallimard. Paris, 1968.

Greenberg, U.Z. *Hagavrut haolah*. Sdan. Tel Aviv, 1926.

Greenberg, U.Z. *Gezamelte verke*. 2 Vol. Magnus Press. Jerusalem, 1979.

Hareven, S. *Ir yamim rabim*. Am Oved. Tel Aviv, 1972.

Herzig, H. *Hashem haperati: masot al yaakov shabtai, yehoshua kenaz, yoel hofman*. Hakibbutz hameuhad. Tel Aviv, 1994.

Hever, H. *Uri tsvi greenberg: taarukhah bimlot lo shmonim*. Hebrew University Library. Jerusalem, 1977.

Hoffmann, Y. *The Idea of Self - East and West*. Firma KLM. Calcutta, 1980.

Hoffmann, Y. *Japanese Death Poems*. CharlesE. Tuttle. Tokyo, 1986.

Hoffmann, Y. *Sefer yosef*. Keter. Jerusalem, 1988.

Hoffmann, Y. *Katschen and the Book of Joseph*. New Directions. New York, 1996.

Hoffmann, Y. *Bernhard*. Keter. Jerusalem, 1989. Bernhard. New Directions. New York, 1998.

Hoffmann, Y. *Christus shel dagim*. Keter. Jerusalem, 1991.

Hoffmann, Y. *Mah shlomekh dolores?* Keter. Jerusalem, 1995.

Horn,S. *Arba imahot*. Maariv. Tel Aviv, 1996.

Hume, D. *A Treatise of Human Nature*. Oxford University Press. Oxford, 1881.

Katzir, J. *Lematis yesh et hashemesh babeten*. Hakibbutz hameuhad. Tel Aviv, 1996.

Kerrett, E. *Tsinorot*. Am Oved. Tel Aviv, 1992.

Kerrett, E. *Gaaguay lekisinger*. Zmorah Bitan. Tel Aviv, 1994.

Kressel, G. *Leksikon lasifrut haivrit*. 2 vol. Sifriat poalim. Tel Aviv, 1965.

Lev, E. *Haboqer harishon began eden*. Keshet. Tel Aviv, 1996.

Levi, P. *Se questo è un uomo*. Ennaudi. Torino, 1958.

Linur, I. *Shirat hasirenah*. Zmorah Bita. Tel Aviv, 1991.

Matalon, R. *Im hapanim elenu*. Am Oved. Tel Aviv, 1996.

Megged, A. *Foiglman*. Am Oved. Tel Aviv, 1987.

Michaels, A. *Fugitive Pieces*. Bloomsbury. London, 1996.

Modiano, P. *La Place de l'étoile*. Gallimard. Paris, 1968.

Modiano, P. *Rue des Boutiques Obscures*. Gallimard. Paris, 1978.

Molco, S. *Sefer hamfoar*. Originally published 1529. Reprinted, Jerusalem, 1993.

Naor, M. ed. *Qesher*. Tel Aviv. May, 1998.

Oz, A. *Oto hayam*. Keter. Jerusalem, 1998.

Proust, M. *A la Récherche du Temps Perdu*. Gallimard. Paris, 1954.

Ramras-Rauch, G. *Aharon Appelfeld: The Holocaust and Beyond*. Indiana University Press. Bloomington, 1994.

Rattok, L. *Bayit al belimah: omanut hasipur shel a.apelfeld*. Heqer. Tel Aviv, 1989.

Ravitch, M. *Dos maaseh buch fun main lebn*. 3 volumes. Verlag I.L. Peretz.

Tel Aviv, 1975.

Schwartz, Y. *Kinat hayahid venetsah hashevet*. Keter. Jerusalem, 1996.

Sebald, W.G. *The Emigrants*. The Harvill Press. London, 1996.

Shaham, N. *Lev tel aviv*. Am Oved. Tel Aviv, 1994.

Shaked, G. *Gal hadash basiporet haivrit*. Sifriat poalim. Tel Aviv, 1970.

Shalev, M. *Roman rusi*. Am Oved. Tel Aviv, 1988.

Shmeruk, C. *A spigl af a shtayn*. Verlag I.L.Peretz. Tel Aviv, 1964.

Simon,L. *Ahad Haam: A Biography*. Jewish Publication Society. Philadelphia, 1960.

Singer, I.B. *Sonim*. Forverts. New York, 1963.

Singer, I.B. *Enemies: A Love Story*. Noonday Press. New York, 1972.

Singer, I.J. *Fun a velt vos is nishto mer*. Originally published, Forverts, 1944.

Singer, I.J. *Of a World that is no more*. The Vanguard Press. New York, 1970.

Steiner, G.*Language and Silence*. Penguin Books. London, 1967.

Suleiman, S.R. ed. *Exile and Creativity*. Duke University Press. Durham, 1998.

Taub, G. *Hamered hashafuf*. Hakibbutz hameuhad. Tel Aviv, 1997.

Wilkomirski, B. *Fragments: Memories of a Childhood, 1939-1948*. Picador. London, 1996.

Young, J. *Writing and Rewriting the Holocaust: Narrative and the Consequences of Interpretation*. Indiana University Press. Bloomington, 1988.

Yudkin, L.I. *Escape into Siege*. Routledge and Kegan Paul. London, 1974.

Yudkin, L.I. *Al shirat atsag*. Rubin Mass. Jerusalem, 1987.

Yudkin, L.I. *Beyond Sequence: Current Israeli Fiction and its Context*. Symposium Press. London, 1992.

Yuter, A. *The Holocaust in Hebrew Literature: From Genocide to Rebirth*. Associated Faculty Press. New York, 1983

INDEX